Is Your Retirement Heading in the Right Direction?

Steven Casto

Certified Senior Advisor (CSA)

& Compass Expert

Important Note

This book discusses various investments, as well as many ways to invest. All illustrations are hypothetical and have been used to illustrate concepts for educational purposes. Please keep in mind that they do not represent a particular investment. These illustrations are included only to illustrate a concept and should not be considered indicative of actual rates or terms available. The market for all securities is subject to fluctuation, and upon sale, an investor may receive more or less than his or her original investment. This book has the understanding that neither the author or publisher are engaged in rendering legal, accounting, or other professional survives by publishing this book.

A Strategic Wealth Solutions book
Steve Casto
(402) 333 -8751
steve@stevecasto.com

Copyright 2005 by Steven Casto 2nd edition
Cover design by Cathi Stevenson
Text design by Ben Monroe
1. Compass™ is a trademark of Compass Financial Tools, LLC.

IBSN 0-9765718-3-8

Contents

Chapter Seven:
Income Planning 103

Chapter Eight:
Tax Strategies 109

Chapter Nine:
Consequences of Using the
Wrong Strategy 125

Tables

Figures

Dedication

I dedicate this book to my wife who is my best friend and has always believed in me, my family for their loving support and my clients who put their trust in me. God bless you all.

In loving memory to
Reba Rainey,
Peggy Rainey,
& Ruthann Sila

Introduction

To give real service you must add something which cannot be bought or measured with money, and that is sincerity and integrity.
-Donald A. Adams

How will my decisions impact my ability to create the peace of mind I desire? Remember: That's what it's all about. It's not about the money *per se*. It's about managing your money in a way that allows you to fulfill your values, achieve your goals, and bridge the gap from where you are now to where you want to be, so you can live the life you've always wanted.

Sit down for a meeting with most financial people, and you are most likely to be asked questions with numerical answers:

- How much do you have invested?
- How much did you earn last year?
- What is the value of the property you own?

While these are important to know, doesn't it make sense to start off with these kinds of questions:

- What is truly important to you?
- What values do you want to live by?
- What is more important in life than money?

Once you understand your *true purpose for money,* a whole different conversation and pattern of investing occurs. It actually leads you to develop a life long game plan to achieve true peace of mind.

That's because a Trusted Advisor (explained in chapter two), represents a very different perspective on managing wealth than a typical salesperson in the industry. Trusted Advisor's pride themselves in developing relationships with their clients that are based on trust and understanding. The content of this book may be the most valuable information you will ever receive for making smart choices with you money! You deserve a Trusted Advisor to help you implement your written financial strategy (Compass™ - explained in chapter one) to achieve your goals and fulfill what is truly important to you (your core values).

In these pages, I hope you will find the clarity and inspiration to achieve all of your financial goals, while fulfilling your highest values and having a great life! The power of choice is in your hands.

COMPASS™ - INCOME FOR LIFE

Are you uncertain about retirement? Do you fear outliving your money? Losing your independence? Reducing your standard of living? Having to rely on your children for assistance? You're not alone. Seventy-five percent of seniors say their number one concern is running out of money.

The truth about retirement is you can have peace of mind and sleep soundly every night secure in the knowledge that you won't outlive your money. You can have the money to fully enjoy the life you've worked so hard for. We can create an ironclad plan for generating an inflation-adjusted income that you won't outlive. **But it takes a plan.**

Do you have enough money for retirement? "Biggest mistakes consumers are making today:

- Underestimating how much income they'll need after they retire.

- Underestimating how long they will live.

- Overestimating how much they can withdrawal from their portfolio without depleting it."[1]

The challenge is we are just living longer. More people are living to age 100 according to the Census Bureau. In fact, for a healthy couple age 65, there is a 55% chance that one person will live to at least age 90[2]. In the long run, you only have two choices with money: either you are going to outlive your money or your money is going to outlive you. Which scenario would you rather have happen to you?

Financial Risks of living longer:

- Not being able to maintain your desired standard of living

- Not keeping up with inflation

- Outliving your assets[3]

Are You Prepared For The Challenge Of Retirement?

- 39% of Americans think they'll have enough money to live comfortably in retirement. *USA Today, 11/16/03*

- 45% of retirees are less secure than they thought they'd be. *LIMRA 2003*

---

[2] Source: "Retirement Storm Clouds," by Walter Updegrave, *CNNMoney*, November 3, 2003

[3] *LIMRA, 1999*

[4] *LIMRA, 2003*

- 74% of Americans rate having retirement income that will last long enough as their #1 goal. *Phoenix/Harris Interactive Wealth Study 2003*

- 78% of Americans do not have a formal written retirement plan. *LIMRA 2003*

- 78% of Americans say they could do more to plan their retirement. *LIMRA 2003*

- 80% of Americans think they'll have to work in retirement. *AARP Study 2003*

The cost of aging is not new. What is new is the length of time you'll have to provide that income. And the longer you live, the more inflation will affect you and the harder it might be to preserve your lifestyle.

In today's highly complex and rapidly changing world, you are faced with an incredible array of investment choices. Many financial people will be happy to help invest your hard earned dollars, but that's just one small part of achieving your overall peace of mind. You have to be careful because virtually everyone is affected by the financial illusions I talk about later. These illusions are destructive and upsetting because they create stress and anxiety in your life.

The Compass™ System will literally put your mind at ease for the rest of your life. The goal is to make certain you can sleep at night. It will let you live a peaceful relaxing life; secure in the knowledge you won't outlive your money.

Do you have enough MONEY for Retirement?

Most retirees don't know because they don't know how much income to take. If you take too much you will run out of money. So a lot of seniors live frugal and never get to really enjoy retirement. Compass™ lets you enjoy retirement again.

Income for Life

Making certain you don't run out of money in retirement is even more important than investment planning. It is the single most important issue to address in retirement. You need a strategy that encompasses three main goals: making sure you don't run out of money in retirement, providing a certain income in retirement and protecting your retirement savings. The Compass™ System gives you an ironclad formula for generating an inflation adjusted income that you won't outlive.

The Compass™ System uses a process of laddering assets into legs. By laddering assets into different legs it is possible to mathematically calculate a monthly income that will not eat into your overall principal. In addition to getting income that will not be outlived, there may be a substantial tax benefit which will increase your after tax spendable income. That means not only income for life, but also the possibility of greater income to spend.

Laddering is a system by which assets are purchased for different legs and liquidated in a mathematically formulated sequence to provide maximum income. Through laddering, income from each leg is generated over a specific period of time. By having only one leg in the payout phase at any given time, the earning potential of the entire portfolio is maximized. At least the last leg in the ladder remains untouched, and is projected to create, at minimum, the return of the initial principal.

The first leg in the ladder is designed for consistent income. We don't want to take a lot of risk in leg one. The middle legs are for generating income down the road when leg one has been depleted. You want higher yielding investments but still not wanting to take a lot of risk. The last leg is where you can see some growth and is the exciting leg for some. You must remember that the last leg still should be long term, diversified and invested prudently. We have taken the time to look at all investments and what makes the most sense for each appropriate leg based on tax consequences, rate of return and risk.

Tax savings may be created for assets not otherwise in a qualified retirement plan by pushing taxable income below the Social Security tax thresholds. Anyone who wants to minimize taxes, thus increasing income will be interested in this. Our country's founders had a tea party long ago to dispute excess tax, yet too many seniors these days are simply unaware that they are being hammered in taxes. Like the IRS's required tax on Social Security benefits and they can tax as much as 85% of your benefits!

This strategy shows you how to get your taxable income below the Social Security Tax Thresholds; how to limit income taxes that result from typical investments; and demonstrates what a before and after 1040 tax form will look like. By reducing taxable income, or income that is countable towards the Social Security thresholds, you will reduce taxes and increase spendable income. Some of the savings are from tax reduction and some are from tax deferral.

In the laddering process, much of the money withdrawn from the first leg is considered return of principle and is therefore tax-free. As the ladder continues over time, more of the withdraws will be taxable. The amount of tax savings will vary based on your Federal Income Tax rate. As an example, the initial income could be withdrawn as high as 90% tax-free.

Laddering assets to create a Compass™ program consists of some guaranteed returns and some assumed returns. You must be extremely careful when preparing your Compass™ program to use the right products in conjunction with the right assumptions.

The Compass™ System is also suitable for planning your Required Minimum Distributions (RMD's) and possible Roth conversions on your IRA.

Remember: It's not what you make...but what you keep that counts!

Compass™ with IRA's

Retirement funds accumulated through 401k, IRA's and other qualified retirement plans demand careful planning and protection. These funds if properly planned and managed, will serve you throughout your retirement years and then pass to your children or grandchildren. Compass™ shows you how to transfer your account without penalties, without tax consequences and with safety. It will also show you proper beneficiary designations to allow your family to stretch the IRA and make sure you don't accidentally disinherit someone.

Beneficiaries are so important because if you are not careful, and have the wrong beneficiaries or use the wrong beneficiary forms, your IRA upon your death could be subject to serious tax surprises. For example, many people name their Trusts as the beneficiaries. If your IRA is liquidated into a trust, that IRA could be taxed at the rate of the trust, which is the highest tax rate today. The federal income tax rate for trusts is 35% once that trust income is over $9,550.

This strategy will also determine if a rollover or transfer is beneficial; shows alternatives such as a Roth Conversion and Stretch applications; and demonstrates how to use IRA money to generate maximum income and minimum tax consequences. In addition, this will help plan Required Minimum Distributions and show you how best to use these funds if they are not needed for income.

If you are leaving a company or retiring from your employer, rolling over a 401k or other retirement account offers greater flexibility and more options in the handling and investment of your retirement money. You will often get a more diverse group of investment choices, many of which may be more appropriate for your needs than you currently are getting. In addition, there are tax saving options, which you may elect to use which are not available with your current program, like the Stretch IRA and Roth IRA.

With the stretch IRA it is possible for your children to take minimum distributions over their lifetime and stretch an IRA for years. By keeping the IRA intact for such a long period of time (through the stretch option) taxes are deferred and money is accumulated at a higher rate due to the affect of triple compounding over a longer period of time. Albert Einstein called this the eighth wonder of the world.

Triple compounding is when you invest your money in a way which allows you to pay no Federal Income Tax, no State Income Tax and the money grows tax deferred. You will receive returns on your principal invested, returns on the returns generated and returns on the dollars not paid in taxes. This power of triple compounding is also available with non-ira money with careful planning.

One of the major benefits is the ability to convert to a Roth IRA. When you convert an IRA to a Roth IRA, taxes become due on the amount converted. With Compass™ you learn which leg or legs you should convert to a Roth IRA. The converted legs grow tax-free and withdrawn totally tax-free by either yourself or your beneficiaries after just five years.   Remember that your adjusted gross income (AGI) must be less than $100,000 for you to convert your IRA into a Roth IRA.

The Compass™ System will help you eliminate the fear of your IRA's value going down 50% or more due to Required Minimum Distributions (RMD's) over your lifetime. You may have looked at the Roth IRA before, but you didn't know the mathematically correct amount to convert. So you just left it alone. Compass™ helps solve the Required Minimum problems as well as the Roth IRA conversion tax problem.

Each Compass™ plan is personally designed based on the amount of money available, income needs, estate needs, health and tax issues. To create a personal Compass™ plan based on your personal goals and circumstances, a personal meeting with a competent person is necessary. Make sure your meeting is without any obligation or cost whatsoever..

You deserve more & you should demand more

What can you expect?

- More income without the fear of outliving it

- Keep better pace with inflation

- Reduce income and estate taxes

- Solve IRA RMD concerns

- Enable you to go on more vacations

- Allow more visits to see the grandchildren

- Maintain a comfortable lifestyle

- Achieve your goals and the *Quality of Life* you envision

A Compass™ Comparison

Laddering assets to create a Compass™ program consists of some guaranteed returns and some assumed returns. You must be careful when preparing a Compass™ plan to use the right products in conjunction with the right assumptions.

Example of a 70-year-old retired couple that is concerned about outliving their money using normal planning strategies. Like a lot of people they were falling to a lot of the illusions that I will talk about shortly. They had no real purpose for money, had no idea how to measure the risk in their portfolio and worse had no peace of mind.

After we discovered together their purpose for money and how to measure risk we took that information and put it into Compass™. They were also able to minimize their tax liability to a minimum based on their situation using a significant amount of tax breaks available. Their tax liability was reduced $3,618 and their social security was being taxed at 85% and was reduced to 32 ½ %. There peace of mind was dramatically improved with the fact that they wouldn't outlive their money. We setup a curriculum program for the next 4 years to keep improving their piece of mind as explained in chapter 2.

Some concerns I hear:

- *Why haven't I heard of this before?* This technique has been used by the informed for years. They don't want you to know about it because they want you to continue buying and selling in you accounts instead of following this plan. By the way, mathematics is illogical to turn you back on.

- *What if I live longer than the Compass™ is designed?* You just take the last leg and create a new one for the length of time desired. You should do this while receiving income from the second leg.

- *What if I die, what will happen to the legs?* Your heirs will receive the assets of the different legs without probate. If you're receiving income from a leg, that income will continue to your heir, as it was setup.

What you don't know can hurt you!

The traditional methods of investing in stocks, bonds and mutual funds in order to accumulate and protect assets is fraught with risk. Are you frustrated with suffering losses on you hard-earned money? Are you tired of listening to people who say they can outguess the market and losing your hard-earned assets? Maybe you are falling for these illusions. I don't want you to think that only the weak minds fall prey. It's easy to fall into these traps when they're so pervasively put out there by the financial community, the media, and the public at large.

Learn what almost **NOBODY** In the Financial Community

WANTS YOU TO KNOW...

FINANCIAL ILLUSIONS

Illusion #1. Gambling with your money.

Because the brokerage community, news programs, mutual funds, and magazines all blur the lines that separate speculating, gambling, and investing, most people are speculating and gambling with their money – and they don't even know it. They actually mistake gambling and speculating for wise investing. There are three types of speculating with your money that you must guard against.

- **Stock picking.** Trying to figure out what the next hot stock or group of stocks is going to be. If you hire a manager who tells you what the best stocks are, such as a mutual fund, that's the same thing as day-trading. In this instance you aren't actually day-trading, but it's the same effect because many of the managers are day-trading with your accounts.

- **Market timing.** When assets are moved in the portfolio, based on a forecast or prediction about the future, this is market timing. Market movements are random. No one knows what the market will do tomorrow or over the next twelve months, and if they did they wouldn't tell you!

- **Past performance.** The last way you know you're gambling and speculating with your money is track record investing. Track record investing entails going with a manager, much like betting on a horse that had stellar performance in the past. Studies show how a manager's ability to pick the best stocks in one period and repeat it in the next period has Zero Correlation.

Illusion #2: Mistaking "stuff" for diversification.

Investors believe that if they have a lot of items on their statement, they are diversified. You might think when you get your statement, "Wow, I'm really diversified. Look at all these companies." For argument's sake, let's say that all of these companies are in one asset category, such as the S&P 500. Given anecdotal evidence, the investor is told by his broker that these are very large and stable companies. What the investor is not told, is that because all of these companies are in only one asset class, that they tend to move in a step-rate fashion, and when one crashes they all tend to crash together. So when the market crashes, chances are the investor is going to lose massive amounts of money.

Illusion #3. Mistaking activity for control.

We're lead to believe that if we buy and sell, we are in control. Here, we must explore the difference between real control and the false sense of control that trading, stock picking, forecasting, and track record investing create. The more active you are in these areas, the more out of control you actually are. Just as in Vegas, the odds are staked against you.

Commercials epitomize the belief that if you buy and sell frequently you will be in control of both your portfolio and your own destiny. It portrays this buying, selling, and speculating glut as healthy and even goes as far as intimating that if you trade at home you can be a better father and family man. Perhaps a more accurate portrayal would highlight an ego-and adrenaline-driven father taking time away from his family to addictively gamble with their futures.

Illusion #4: Believing that this time it is different.

In the late 1990's, we were lead to believe by the brokerage community, newspapers, media, the TV shows and the financial magazines that we were in a "new paradigm." It went something like this… "We are in a new paradigm, and because the Internet is the most powerful technology known to mankind, it will shape the future of business and investing. It will reshape reality. It seemed like good logic. This new brand of investing seemed to offer all of the upside potential with a low probability of loss. That risk and return were no longer related. It seemed like a "sure thing."

This new belief and the allure of high returns with low risk caused investors to give up true diversification in favor of narrowly cast portfolios in one or two asset categories. It seemed to be the proverbial goose that laid the golden egg.

But this is not the first time that this has happened. This is the same thing that happened in the Great Depression and to poor Isaac Newton when he lost all of his money in the South Sea bubble. You might remember that Isaac Newton discovered gravity and invented differential calculus. Even a true genius can get caught up in this.

Illusion #5: Believing all risk is equal.

In my belief, taking risk for its own sake is a crime in and of itself because it puts you in a position where your capacity to live fully and to enjoy your wealth is greatly diminished.   Why would you ever do that?

A form of this is ignoring the sum of all outcomes when investing or Worse Case Scenario. A worse case scenario means studying and analyzing all of the possible negative outcomes and factoring that into your decision making process. By incorporating this into your process, you can separate prudent risk-taking from imprudent risk-taking. In other words, separate true investing from rank speculation.

"Is controlling risk important to you?" Most investors will answer "yes" to this question – as it should be. But even though every investor knows risk is important, few indeed, can answer my next question successfully. "Can you show me an academic number, a statistic that shows the amount of risk and volatility in your portfolio?" When I ask this question I am usually greeted with silence.

Then I hit them with the next question. "Well, if you can't actually measure risk in any meaningful way, is there any way that you can control it? And, of course, the next answer is a resounding – "NO." What this often leads to are big losses in their portfolios.

Illusion #6: The "I'll stop when I get even" reflex.

When is the best time to be prudent? Most investors respond, "It is always the right time to be prudent." And they're exactly right.

If imprudent risk-taking and speculation has cost you money, the worst thing that you could do is participate in imprudent, speculative, and risk-taking activities going into the future. So why do people often insist on continuing with the imprudent behavior? For many people, it is easier to make a bad decision even worse by continuing the destructive process than to face it head on.

You need to realize that you are not your decisions, and just because you made an improper, or imprudent decision in the past, does not mean that you are less of a person, or less intelligent. As a matter of fact, it's a sign of intelligence and growth to solve and put an end to a destructive process when you become aware that it exists.[5]

A solution to these illusions is to harness the power of free markets by owning structured market portfolios that are designed to deliver market rates of return and minimize risk. These are typically available to only the most sophisticated investors.

---

[5] Courtesy of Mark Matson, © 2005 McGriff Publishing. The Investor Awareness Guide

"Go confidently in the direction
of your dreams!
Live the Life you've Imagined"

-Thoreau

ENHANCE YOUR QUALITY OF LIFE

**"When your values are clear,
your decisions are easy." Roy Disney**

Peace of mind: What is it? How can we find it?

These are questions that plaque most investors. For multiple reasons, many people don't believe it is even possible to feel peaceful about investing. Learn strategies designed to help you overcome investing frustrations and achieve peace of mind about your financial future. These strategies eliminate massive confusion and anxiety by posing the right questions and help you find the answers that are right for you.

Conscious investing for Peace of Mind is a fun introduction to all the concepts in the curriculum and offers the opportunity to better understand what we call "the human side of investing." Take the Conscious Investor Quiz (if you have never heard or seen this before call or email me immediately to get a copy), learn the Conscious Investor Formula, and begin to ask the "right" questions about investing.

This curriculum is something we use with our clients over a 4-5 year span. The workbooks are used to gradually increase understanding and develop a strong relationship between investor and advisor. As you complete this well-designed, step-by-step process, you will find that it leads to high mutual trust levels and the ability to focus on what is most important to you – *your* lifelong goals.

The Curriculum for Conscious Investing includes:

- **Discovering your True Purpose for Money.** True Purpose for Money is the crucial first step that paves the way for long-lasting satisfaction and fulfillment about financial decisions. Find out how you've been trapped in the Investors' Dilemma, and then reveal your own True Purpose for Money.

- **Choosing your Investment Philosophy.** A solid, well-understood investment philosophy provides a stable foundation upon which to base future decisions. This is one of the most important – but usually overlooked – aspects of investing.

- **Defeating your Money Demons.** Locked within each of use are deeply rooted belief systems about money and what it means. Some of the beliefs are negative and can be at the core of unhappiness about personal financial issues. When you bring your Money Demons to the level of awareness, you can defeat them and create new beliefs that lead to different actions and outcomes.

- **Understanding the Dimensions of Risk & Return.** The terms "risk" and "return" have different meanings to different people. It's easy to get confused. Understanding the Dimensions of Risk and Return clarifies these frequently talked about, yet rarely understood, concepts of investing.

- **Focusing on your Future View.** Deliberately reveal what is most important so you can clearly focus on making your dreams come true. You will shed new light on what it is you want money to accomplish. In this way, you re-define your own investment "success."

- **Examining Your Expectations.** Begin to understand the relationship between expectations and results and you will see that it is crucial to peace of mind about investing. No matter what it is in life, your expectations are the deciding factor in how you feel about the outcome

- **Creating you Core Covenants.** Relationships are critical not only to success in families, in business and in sports, but also to the overall quality of life. Creating core covenants is a strategy designed to help individuals deliberately build strong relationships in any setting.

- **Customizing your Lifelong Gameplan.** The final component walks you through a clear process so you can integrate and customize all of the personal information you have revealed throughout the curriculum. Your Lifelong

Gameplan is a comprehensive, cohesive document that brings the components of your investing future together.

- **How the Really Smart Money Invests (video).** This award-winning video reveals what Nobel Prize winners have discovered about the nature of the market, and explains how people who are highly educated in the field utilize this information to invest their own money. It also details why investors often become enmeshed in the emotional side of investing, as well as how to make smart decisions on a consistent basis about how you invest your money.

Completing the Curriculum for Conscious Investing allows you to leverage your ability to take precise meaningful action, achieve greater results, and experience peace of mind about your money.

I'd like to add that when your values are clear and you know what you need to do to fulfill them…and you realize there are only a finite number of hours in the day, the decision to delegate what you can is easy. Nobody wastes their lives days, weeks, months or years at a time. It's fifteen minutes here…a half-hour there…a few hours occasionally … that are easily wasted. I strongly encourage you to consider delegating what you can so you can focus your time on what's important to you.

Here are some things to consider about your Peace of Mind:

1. Do you know what a P/E ratio is but not an HDL/LDL ratio?

2. Do you know how many stars your mutual fund has, but have no idea about your body fat percentage?

3. Are you more likely to read Money magazine this week than the Bible?

4. Will you spend more time this week watching financial shows on TV than praying?

5. Did you sign more proxy cards for your stocks and mutual funds than birthday cards for your friends and family?

Let your Trusted Advisor spend his or her time managing your money, so you can enjoy the things you value most in your life. Life Advisors who specialize in Money = Trusted Advisors.

Salesperson or Trusted Advisor? Which Would You Choose to Handle Your Money?

A Trusted Advisor...

- Has a structured process for creating a comprehensive financial plan for clients.

- Is interested in what's important to you and wants to listen to your significant issues

- Requires that you bring all your financial data to the first meeting, but does not require that you disclose any information until you are comfortable

- Expresses interest in and refers frequently to the work you have done to prepare for the first meeting, and helps prepare your True Purpose for Money in an effort to understand your values and goals.

- Is happy to refer you to someone else if he or she senses there is not a good match.

- Meets with you in a professional environment and requires that anyone who shares financial decisions and responsibilities be present.

- Inspires you in a positive way.

- Won't be talked into just selling you a product...even if you insist.

A Salesperson...

- Has a technique for making the sale.

- Engages you in small talk, chitchat or banter designed to relax you and establish rapport with you.

- Does not require that you do anything other than show up to the first meeting. Has low standards.

- Refers to your impending demise in an attempt to scare you into buying a product to fill a need.

- Will tell you that he or she can (and will) work with anybody.

- Will meet with anyone, anywhere, anytime in the name of "convenience," which is actually a sign of desperation.

- Tends to prey on your fears and insecurities to get you to "buy."

- Will sell you anything you want to buy…or will simply redirect you to a preferred product.[7]

A Trusted Advisor helps you make the wise decisions about how much volatility, and what types of risk you want to incorporate into your portfolio. Most salespeople do not get paid for being prudent, they get paid for selling products.

A Trusted Advisor along with Compass™ is different from traditional financial planning. It is a process designed to help you overcome investing frustrations and achieve peace of mind about your financial future.

---

[7] Parts of this chapter courtesy of Bill Bachrach, ©2000 Bill Bachrach, Values-Based Financial Planning™ and Values-Based Selling®, at (www.valuesbasedfinancialplanning.com) and Abundance Technologies, Inc. 2001.

Mistakes Made in IRA's & 401k's Can Cost You a Fortune

You've heard of the expression, "Learn by your mistakes." Well, I am a big believer that it is cheaper to learn by other people's mistakes! Retirement accounts (IRAs, 403bs, 457 plans etc.) are very complicated and few people realize this.

Compass™ will determine if a rollover is necessary; show alternatives such as Roth Conversions and Stretch applications; and demonstrates how to use IRA's for maximum income with minimum tax consequences. If you are not using Compass™ make sure to read this chapter thoroughly because one little mistake can cost you thousands of dollars.

Over 4000 people each day reach age 70 ½ and by law, must start their IRA distributions (or pay severe IRS penalties). You must make some difficult technical decisions about your IRA.

- Who should be the "designated" beneficiary?
- When should a trust be used as a beneficiary?
- Should there be a separate IRA for each beneficiary?
- Should money be left to charity from the IRA?

A few other questions that any serious IRA owner should ask their financial person to make sure they are up to the task:

- What resources do they use to stay up to date on changing IRA rules? (They should be at arm's length)
- What was the last IRA ruling they were aware of? (On average one a week)
- When was the last time they attended an IRA training session? (Have them show you the manual)

But when you know the details, you can earn more on your retirement plan, pay less tax on withdrawals, avoid common mistakes in naming your beneficiaries and get more financial benefits.

Convert to a Roth IRA Using Compass™

If your income is less than $100,000 and you have a retirement plan over $100,000, you should take the time to look at what Compass™ can do with IRA money.

It would create two sources of money, part in the IRA account and part to convert to a Roth IRA. Your IRA grows tax deferred and your Roth grows tax-free!!! You would transfer part to a Roth IRA based on what Compass™ tells you and keep the rest in the IRA account. You would use your IRA account first for current needs, realizing that each withdrawal is taxable. Over the years after your IRA account has been depleted, you are left with your Roth IRA account, which has been growing tax-free and has no required distributions. So now when you need income from the Roth IRA, you can get it tax-free by tapping the Roth.

Additionally, the Roth is an excellent choice for your family in that the Roth can be inherited income tax free and grows income tax-free for up to two more generations (through your grandchildren's life).

Like the idea of tax free social security! By replacing taxable IRA distributions with tax free Roth distributions, you reduce your taxable income which may allow you to qualify for tax-free social security benefits.

Worried about the increased tax brackets that single (widowed) people face? Replace taxable IRA distributions with tax-free Roth distributions. No matter how high your tax bracket is, Roth distributions are income tax free. Please don't try this without first looking at Compass™.

Don't Disinherit Your Grandkids

(And Why You Need Special Beneficiary-Designation Form)

Let's say you have two sons, Sam and Bob. You name them as primary beneficiaries for your IRA when you open the account by completing an "IRA Beneficiary Designation Form."

As shown at the top of the following page, Sam and Bob each have a daughter. Sam's daughter is Sue. Bob's daughter is Angie. So you put your granddaughter's names on the line of the beneficiary designation form that says "secondary beneficiaries."

Table 3.1
Don't Let Your Custodian Mess You Up

Primary Beneficiaries: Your Sons	Jack	Tom
Secondary Beneficiaries: Your Grandsons	Bob	Dan

If Jack dies before you do, what happens to Jack's half of your IRA when you pass away? You probably think it goes to his son, Bob. Wrong.

It goes to Tom, because on your beneficiary designation form, there is no place to specify how the primary beneficiaries and secondary beneficiaries were related. There is no place for you to explain your intentions and your desires with respect to those beneficiaries. Those beneficiary designation forms that you filled out with the bank or the securities firm may not be sufficiently detailed to carry out your probable wishes.

What's the solution? Give your IRA custodian complete instructions on your own form. These forms are known as "Special Designation Forms" because they provide complete set of instructions regarding your retirement assets.

By the way, some retirement plan custodians may refuse to take your custom instructions. If you encounter that, we can assist you in finding a custodian that will accept your instructions. And since retirement assets are freely transferable from custodian to custodian in most cases, you simply move your accounts. The same flexibility applies to a beneficiary who inherits an IRA and finds that the custodian has a rule to payout the IRA quickly rather than allow the stretch concept. The beneficiary can just transfer to a more flexible custodian.

Company Stock in Your 401(k)

Many retirees have employer stock in their 401(k) and profit sharing plans. In these cases, there is an opportunity for converting ordinary income (which could be taxed at rates up to 35% federal plus state) into capital gains income (taxed at only 15% federal plus state).

Here's how: Rather than rolling over the employer stock into an IRA, take actual distribution of the shares. You will pay tax (at ordinary income rates) on the basis of that stock. The basis is the value of the shares when they were originally put into the plan. When you eventually sell the shares, you will be taxed on the unrealized appreciation as a capital gain. If you rollover the shares into an IRA, you would pay ordinary income on the entire value of the shares, since they are withdrawn from the IRA.

Let's look at an example. Joe has a 401(k) plan at ABC Manufacturing. He invests his contributions into company stock during his tenure—a total hypothetical investment of $100,000. When Joe is ready to retire, the shares are worth a hypothetical $600,000. Let's first assume that Joe rolls over the shares into an IRA. He then reaches age 70½ and must begin taking distributions from his IRA and paying taxes on those withdrawals at ordinary income rates (up to 35% federal plus state). He will pay these full rates on all of his shares. Assuming no further appreciation above the

$600,000, Joe would pay tax of $210,000 on the shares (at the 35% federal rate plus state).

But let's assume that Joe read this chapter. Instead of rolling over the shares, he takes them as a distribution and pays tax of $35,000 immediately on the basis (35% of $100,000). Later, he decides to sell the stock (at his discretion because he is not subject to the age 70½ rule because the shares are not in an IRA), and he pays a capital gains tax of $75,000 (15% federal tax of $500,000).

His total federal tax bill is $110,000 rather than the $231,600 he would have paid if he rolled his shares into an IRA. That's a cool savings of $120,000 in federal tax—enough to pay for plenty of great vacations for Joe and his wife.

Are you retiring in the next three years? If so, don't miss out on the many planning opportunities that the mutual fund companies did not explain or your CPA forgot to mention.

Use the New Distribution Rules

Up until the IRS changed the rules on January 11, 2001, seniors were forced to start taking distributions from their IRAs on an irrevocable schedule upon reaching age 70½. Many people did not need or want to take these distributions that increased their taxable income and taxes. However, the IRS wanted to collect taxes and thus the forced distributions. Now, the withdrawals are still forced, but at a lower rate and the IRS will collect less tax during the IRA owner's lifetime.

In addition, the new rules allow IRA owners to change beneficiaries after they start taking distributions (not allowed under old rules) and when the beneficiary inherits the IRA, they can spread the IRA payments over their lifetimes (allowed only for spouses under prior rules). The bottom line: IRA accounts will be allowed to grow over longer periods of time (two generations or more) and the IRS tax take will be deferred for many years—for people who take advantage of the new rules that is.

Take a look at the old tables as compared to the new tables below:[8]

Age	Old Tables Single Life Expectancy	New Tables
71	15.3	26.5
72	14.6	25.6
73	13.9	24.7
74	13.2	23.8
75	12.5	22.9
76	11.9	22
77	11.2	21.2
78	10.6	20.3
79	10.0	19.5
80	9.5	18.7

The table above shows the number you divide into your IRA balance to calculate your distribution. For example, an age 71 male with a $100,000 IRA would need to withdraw $6,536 ($100,000/15.3). Under the new tables, he needs to withdraw only $3,773 ($100,000/

8 IRS Publication 590, 2003.

26.5). At a 25% federal tax rate, he saves $690.

The other big change to your benefit is the ability to change designated beneficiaries. Although many IRA owners did not realize this before, once you started taking mandatory distributions, you were locked into the IRA beneficiaries you had selected. Now, you can change designated beneficiaries anytime, even after death (additional rules apply)! You can give the person settling your estate (your executor or successor trustee) the right to change the designated beneficiary. This may be a flexible tool as the beneficiaries' situations may have changed significantly between the time you named them as beneficiary and the time the estate is settled.

60 Day Rule

Many employers' retirement plans allow for loans to participants. Although IRS provisions allow for loans, some employers opt not to include this provision in order to ease their administrative burden. There are limits on the size of the loans that can be obtained.

Once you roll over the plan balance to your own IRA or Keogh account, you may not take any loans or pledge the retirement accounts as collateral for a loan (if you do, they become taxable). You can, however, use your IRA as a temporary source of liquidity, particularly if you split it into pieces.

Let's assume that you have $200,000 in an IRA. You can withdraw the balance and avoid paying taxes, as long as you return the funds within 60 days to that

IRA or a new IRA account. (Limited to once per calendar year.)

In another scenario, you can take the $200,000 IRA and split it into four $50,000 IRAs. Then you can take $50,000 from the first IRA. Within 60 days, you can replenish that $50,000 by taking the $50,000 from the second IRA and so on with the four IRAs. In this manner, you have extended the 60-day rule into the 240-day rule (four IRAs x 60 days each) to give yourself a longer loan period. (Note that the rollover may only be once each calendar year for each IRA account.)

Don't Let the IRS Be the Beneficiary of Your IRA

Large IRAs face the double whammy of income and estate tax. Without proper planning, the combined tax could exceed 80%. *The Individual Retirement Account Answer Book* by Panel Publishers illustrates an example of a $2 million IRA exposed to taxes.

NY State Death Taxes (16%)	$ 320,000
Net Federal Estate Tax (39%)	$ 780,000
Net Income Tax (43% combined federal and state)	$ 533,099
Total Taxes	$ 1,633,099
Beneficiaries Receive	**$ 366,901**
(18.3% of Original IRA)	

What can you do to avoid this excessive taxation?

1. Take distributions from your IRA and spend it.

2. Take distributions from your IRA and make gifts ($11,000 per year/per donee or $22,000 per donee if you are married).

3. Take distributions from your IRA and contribute the money as premiums for life insurance and have the tax-free death benefit offset the above taxes.

4. Use your IRA (rather than other assets) for charitable bequests or to establish a testamentary charitable remainder trust.

5. Distribute your IRA and contribute the balance to a charitable family limited partnership to offset the tax (see the tax section of this book).

From *Kiplinger's Retirement Report* of August 1999, comes the following advice:

> "Plan for estate taxes. If you have a large IRA and few other liquid assets, consider using required distributions to pay for second-to-die life insurance premiums. This insurance pays on the death of the second spouse and is usually owned by an irrevocable life insurance trust or the IRA's beneficiary so that insurance proceeds stay out of your estate. (A single person can also use a life-insurance trust to pay estate taxes.) 'Whatever you take out of the IRA for premiums, you've removed from your taxable estate and replaced with an estate-tax-free asset," points out Edward Slott, a

CPA in Rockville Centre, N.Y."

If this applies to your situation, then do not wait! The IRS is very happy to take taxes from people who procrastinate. Any one or combination of the above options is better than leaving your IRA as tax fodder.

Should You Spend Non-IRA Money First

You own two pots of money: The money that has already been taxed (let's call it "regular money") and the money that has not been taxed (let's call this "retirement money" such as IRA, 401k, 403b, etc.). When you spend a dollar of regular money, the cost to you is exactly $1. When you spend $1 of retirement money, the cost to you is about $1.33[9] because you need to pay approximately 33% of income tax on the amount you withdraw. Therefore, if you want to reduce your taxes, never take more than the required distribution from your retirement money, even if it means you must spend your regular principal for living expenses.

Some people think they should never spend their principal, but this is a mistake if you want to save taxes. They think that their interest is separate from their principal. But if you look at the money in your pocket, it's all green. Interest and principal are just ideas, and when you look in your bank account you cannot tell which is which. Therefore, it is better to spend your regular principal that has already been taxed and allow your <u>untaxed retirement money to grow as much as possible.</u>

[9] Assumes a combined rate of 28% federal and 5% state which applies to single filers earning $70,350 and married filing jointly earning $117,250 in 2004.

You will be better off financially from an income tax standpoint. Your lifetime tax bill will be less or you will at least defer taxes for many years.

As you can see from the table below, starting with $200,000, you can have $150,000 more by spending your regular money and holding on to your retirement money. Yes, you will eventually pay tax on your IRA money later in life when you use it, or your heirs will pay the tax when you are deceased. But the good news is you get to hold on to more while you're alive.

Table 3.2
Spend Regular Money First

	Today	In 20 Years
Spend Regular Money First		
Regular Money	$100,000	$40,916
IRA Money	$100,000	$320,713
TOTAL	**$200,000**	**$361,629**
Spend IRA Money First		
IRA Money	$100,000	$0
Regular Money	$100,000	$211,247
TOTAL	**$200,000**	**$211,247**

Assumptions: All money earns 6%, combined federal and state income tax is 33%, illustration over 20 years, distributions of $6,000 annually, tax on IRA withdrawals also deducted from IRA account, mandatory IRA distributions not assumed.

Don't Let Your Custodian Ruin Your Plans

If you've consulted a financial advisor about your IRA, they have told you about the "stretch" IRA—the concept of allowing your beneficiaries to spread out the tax on the portion of your retirement dollars that you leave to them. Continuing from our previous hypothetical table, if your $100,000 retirement fund grew to $320,000 and you died before spending any, your heirs would receive the $320,000. They can then make small withdrawals each year (required by IRS) and if the account was inherited by a 42-year-old beneficiary, assuming a hypothetical annual return of 6% and minimum required distributions (IRS Publication 590) would appreciate to $1.3 million during their lifetime.

This sounds great but it may never happen. The two things that can ruin this are your heirs and your IRA custodian.

At your death, your heirs can remove the whole balance in one lump sum and go buy a yacht. Yes, they will pay all of the tax at once and lose years of tax deferral. The way to control this is not to leave your IRA assets outright to heirs, but to leave the assets in an IRA trust. In a trust, you can control how the heir gets paid.

The other problem is that your IRA custodian may ruin your plans by inadvertently acting against your wishes. Your custodian may have rules such as "all distributions to heirs must be paid out in 10 years." If your funds are in a 401k, the plan may also force a fast payout and make the stretch concept impossible to implement for non-spouse beneficiaries.

Beneficiaries Mistakes

When most people select beneficiaries for their IRAs, they select their spouse or their children. As simple as this seems, it can create problems. Consider these two scenarios.

When you leave an IRA account to your spouse, it inflates his or her assets. And if he or she later dies with an estate exceeding $1.5 million (the estate exemptions limits in 2004 and 2005), they pay estate tax. By leaving them your IRA, you have created unnecessary estate taxes by making their estate larger.

If instead you leave the IRA to your son, he may withdraw the funds immediately and decide to buy a mansion jointly with his spouse. Let's say that the following week, your daughter-in-law files for divorce and gets to keep the mansion in the settlement. You just gave your ex-daughter-in-law a mansion with your IRA money.

To avoid the above two scenarios, you decide to leave your IRA to your estate. Based on the IRS's position[10] that an IRA owner's estate cannot be classified as a designated beneficiary, one of the nation's foremost authorities on IRAs advises that you never leave your retirement plan to your estate.[11] At your death, the IRS requires the account to be rapidly distributed rather than enjoy the potential stretch over the lifetimes of beneficiaries. Additionally, the IRA will now be a probate asset and subject to claims of creditors.

---

[10] Private Letter Ruling 2001-26041.
[11] Natalie B. Choate, *Life and Death Planning for Retirement Benefits*, 2003 edition.

So what do rich people do to avoid the three scenarios above? They leave their IRA in a trust and appoint a trustee like an accountant, financial advisor, attorney, etc., a person that has common sense and tax knowledge.

Within the boundaries of your wishes and IRS-required minimum distributions, the trustee is empowered to decide who among your beneficiaries will get the IRA and how much they get. The trustee is empowered to decide how quickly this money gets distributed over and above the annual minimum amount of required IRS distributions. You can even give very detailed instructions.   Or if the money is to be used for education you may stipulate that up to $15,000 a year can be distributed, or to start a business up to $25,000 can be distributed, and you can go on and on with such instructions.

So if you would like to have restrictions or limitations on how your retirement plan eventually gets used and distributed, you should leave it to a trust rather than directly to a person. Because if you leave it to a person, it's their decision how to use it as they desire. To speak to a qualified attorney about having your retirement funds left in trust, contact us for local referrals.[12]

Don't Let Estate Taxes Eat Up Your Retirement Money

Many people have reached age 70½ and are taking only

---

[12] The cost of establishing an IRA trust or IRA asset will varies by location and attorney and may be significant.

the minimum required distributions from their IRAs. By taking only the minimum requirement, their income taxes are minimized. But this tactic can create another problem. If only the minimum amounts are being taken, the IRA balance continues to grow and it could be subject later to double taxation—income and estate taxes.

Many retirees have benefited from increasing home values and investment values in the 1980s and 1990s. As a result, some estates have grown and may be subject to estate tax. IRAs could be subject to two levels of taxes—income tax (rates up to 35% in 2004) and estate tax (rates up to 48% in 2004). But there is a way to offset the threat of this double whammy.

Let's take the hypothetical example, a single IRA owner age 70. He has a 17-year life expectancy.[13] Assume he has a $1 million IRA and takes only the minimum distributions each year so as not to increase his income taxes. Assume the IRA earns a hypothetical 10% annually. Based on these hypothetical assumptions, by life expectancy, that IRA balance will be $2,315,270.[14] Assuming he has no other assets, the IRA will be subject to income tax at rates up to 35% and estate tax up to 48%.

---

[13] IRS Publication 590, 2003.
[14] Calculated by growing the balance each year by a hypothetical 10% and distributing the required minimum distributions per IRS Publication 590, 2003.

Plan Balance	$2,315,720
Income Tax (33% assumed for this example)	$764,187 [15]
Estate Tax (2004 IRS rates)	$ 376,545 [16]
Net to Heirs	$1,174,988

In this example, 50% of the IRA value is lost to taxes. By taking only minimum distributions and saving income taxes today, our investor could create a huge estate tax problem for tomorrow. The total tax can be reduced with some advanced planning.

If instead of taking only the minimum distribution, our IRA owner distributes an additional $19,373 annually from his IRA (and pays the additional tax of $6,393 based on a combined tax bracket of 28% federal and 5% state). He invests the remaining after-tax amount of $12,980 in a fixed universal life policy owned outside of his estate.[17] At his death, he leaves his heirs a death benefit of $500,000, which is free of estate and income taxes.[18] Of course, the IRA balance will also be smaller due to the distributions to pay for the life insurance.

---

[15] This income tax may not be payable all at once as proper beneficiary designations may allow the tax to be paid over the life of the beneficiaries.

[16] Estate tax based on total estate of $2,315,720. Estate tax on income in respect of a decedent can be recovered by the heirs.

[17] The purchase of life insurance may involve significant expenses, fees, and surrender charges. Not everyone can qualify for life insurance and such qualification and rate is based on health. If the policy is deemed to be a modified endowment contract, distributions of earnings are taxable.

[18] Current interest rate of 5.5%, continuous annual payments of $12,980 based on nonsmoker preferred rating provides a death benefit of $500,000 free of estate and income tax if properly purchased and owned outside the insured's estate, First Penn Pacific Titan One, 3/9/04.

Plan Balance	$1,810,637
Income Tax	$597,510
Estate Tax (2004 IRS rates)	$139,786
Life Insurance death benefit	$500,000
Net to Heirs	$1,573,341 [19]

If your current plans involve leaving an IRA to your family, you may leave them better off if this technique fits your situation.

What Investments Should Be in Your IRA?

Which investments should be in your IRA and which outside your IRA to help reduce your taxes? Inside your IRA you want to have growth mutual funds if you own them.

The average growth mutual fund has a turnover rate exceeding 100% a year.[20] In order to get the most favorable capital gains treatment on stock gains, a fund must hold a stock for more than 12 months. But these high-turnover funds are holding many stocks for less than 12 months. The gains on stocks which are turned over before 12 months are "short-term" gains and the maximum tax on short-term gains can be as high as 35%, federal rather than the maximum "long-term"

---

[19] This technique may not be beneficial in every situation. Death benefit in above example assumed to pay off after 17 years, the life expectancy of a 70-year-old. The actual results will vary depending on actual lifetime, actual health rating, actual tax rates, and earnings on the IRA.

[20] The average turnover of stocks categorized as "domestic stock funds" was 124% in 2003. Data from Morningstar Principia Pro, 12/31/03.

capital gains tax of 15%. Therefore, high turnover and high tax funds are best held inside your IRA where you will be shielded from tax.

Table 3.3
Investment Options

INSIDE IRA	OUTSIDE IRA
Growth Mutual Funds	Index/Low Turnover Mutual Funds
Short-Hold Stocks	Long-Hold Stocks
Taxable Bonds	Tax-Free Bonds

Keep low turnover mutual funds, such as index funds, outside of your IRA. Keep stocks you are holding for the long term outside of your IRA. Gains on both investments are taxed mostly at 15%.

If you realize that you may have the wrong items in or out of your IRA, we can show you how to make changes to bring your retirement money and your regular money into balance for lower taxes.

Maybe You Should Convert to a Roth IRA When the Market is Down

Most people have heard of the Roth IRA but few seniors have converted their regular IRAs. And that's understandable, as the tax on the conversion becomes immediately due. However, if the investments held in your IRA have lost value then it may be time to give this option your full attention.

When your IRA balance is down, you can convert to a Roth IRA, pay your tax on a reduced value, and future distributions are tax free. (For the first five years after conversion you may withdraw principal tax free, but earning withdrawals would be subject to tax. If under age 59½, all withdrawals are also subject to penalty.) Not everyone can take advantage of the Roth conversion, as your adjusted gross income must be under $100,000. If your adjusted gross income exceeds $100,000, you may be able to make adjustments to drop your income for one year. For example, those people with a business or income in their control may be able to defer income, drop their income for one year, and make the Roth conversion.

This conversion is best for people who prefer to have growth-oriented investments in their IRA and plan to take advantage of much of their balance during their lifetime. (If you plan to leave much of your IRA in your estate, see the more powerful strategy on "Don't let Estate Taxes Eat Up Your Retirement Money.")

There are additional benefits to tax-free distributions from a Roth IRA. First, there are no required minimum distributions as with a regular IRA. Additionally, you may pay less tax on your Social Security income. Since the tax on Social Security income is calculated on your total income (minus distributions from a Roth IRA), you may experience additional tax savings from a Roth conversion.

Also, if you are married, it is common that the household income remains the same when one spouse dies. This often pushes the single spouse into a higher tax bracket (because single people are taxed more heavily than married people on the same income). By having a Roth IRA, the tax-free distributions may help a surviving spouse qualify for a lower tax bracket.

Would the Roth IRA benefit you? We can do a free comparison of keeping your regular IRA or converting to the Roth with Compass™.

LIVING LONGER

The 20th century retirees are living longer than any previous generation. And the next generation will live longer yet. This could mean that many recently retired couples may expect to need an income for 30 to 40 years.

Do I have enough money to last because I may live to 100? Sounds great. But what are the downsides? "How can there be downsides?" you may ask. After all, you'd have more time to golf, go fishing, and spend with the grandkids. Well, the risk may be that if you hadn't planned to live that long you could end up running out of money.

So how long of a retirement should you plan for? According to the IRS, a 70-year old person is expected to live for 17 more years to age 87. However, this is an average. Half of the 70-year olds will live longer and half will not. Therefore, a 70-year old individual who is basing his or her retirement plan and spending habits on living to 87 is rolling the dice. Furthermore, when you consider that there are more than 70,000 U.S. centenarians who represent the fastest-growing segment of our population, there is reason to take notice.

However, planning too conservatively could be detrimental as well. After all, you don't want to cut your standard of living down to the point that you'll be miserable. And of course, you always have the option to make adjustments in your spending as time goes on. All of this comes down to two simple facts: You can control how long your money will last, but you only have a limited ability to predict how long you will live. So what can you do to reduce the risk of running out of money too soon?

A Compass offers an income that will continue for a lifetime, no matter how long you live. And it will help you plan for the possibility of living to 87, 107, or beyond.

Life Expectancies

In the long run, you only have two choices with money: either you are going to outlive your money or your money is going to outlive you. Which scenario would you rather have happen to you? Although most people would like both to expire on the same day, that's unlikely. The table at the top of the next page shows how long people tend to live.

Table 4.1
Life Expectancies

CURRENT AGE	LIFE EXPECTANCY
55	84.6
60	85.2
65	86.0
70	87.0
75	88.4
80	90.2
85	92.6
90	95.5
95	99.1
100	102.9

Source: IRS Publication 590, 2002.

The average person who is now 73 years old will live to age 87. That's 14 years. So, if the average 73-year-old buys a 15-year bond that would not be too long. Make sure your money lasts as long as you do—try to secure long-term investments, which tend to pay more (with rare exceptions). The best way to preserve your principal is to make your money earn as much as possible, because the more it earns, the less chance you're ever going to have to touch the capital.

The life expectancy table is probably too conservative. This table is historical and reflects the longevity of people born decades ago. In other words, based on historical fact, a person who reaches age 73 on average will live until age 87. For those of you reading this book, those numbers are even higher. The table on this page contains data for people who have already died. But the life expectancy trend is still accurate today. The table shows what's happened to life expectancy and what continues to occur. The bad news (financially anyway) is that life expectancy keeps increasing!

Figure 4.2
The Rising Tide of Life Expectancies (1900-2004)

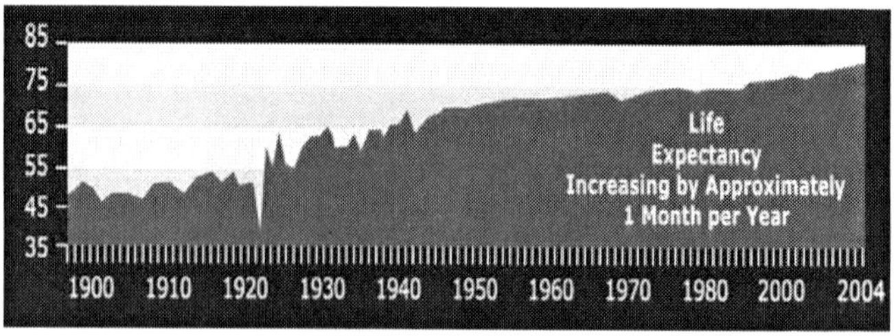

Source: Center for Disease Contol, 2004.

In 1850, the average person lived approximately 37 years. In 1900, that number rose to 47 years. Notice that this chart keeps climbing at about one month of additional life expectancy per year. It doesn't seem to slow down. Doctors are very good at getting us to live longer. So, that's the good news. The bad news is that you need more money. It's a double-edged sword.

Think long term. You are probably going to be around longer than you think, so thinking long term will help you. As a passing note, the big difference between rich and poor people is that rich people think about the long term, while poor people focus on the short term.

Inflation

Although inflation was not such a big problem in the old days when people did not live very long in retirement, it is a critical issue for those of us who will today. In a sense, it is the increase in life expectancies that causes us to be so much more concerned about inflation. Today's retirees will need to protect themselves against the ravages of inflation for very long retirement periods. You must have a good sense for historical inflation rates. You should be aware that even though past inflation rates cannot predict future rates, they can be an important guide in making reasonable assumptions about the future. Ultimately, retirees must work with their financial advisors to determine inflation rates that make sense in their own particular circumstances.

Even a cursory look at the consequences of inflation over future 30-year retirement periods using historical inflation rates is enough to sensitize you toward this critical issue. The price of a loaf of bread, using the 25-year average annual rate of inflation between 1974 and 1998, 5.2 percent, will increase from about $2.50 today to almost $11.50 in 30 years.[21] A retiree who wants to maintain a $50,000 lifestyle in today's dollars at the five-year average annual inflation rate of only 2.4 percent between 1994 and 1998 must increase his or her income to over $100,000 by the end of a typical 30-year retirement period. The question then is "In even the best of circumstances, what provisions have you made in your financial plans to double your income over the next 30 years?"

While answering this question, retirees must remember that since they will be retired, the entire increase will have to come out of their retirement portfolios. Ultimately, everyone needs to decide for themselves (with help from advisors) what inflation rates to build into his or her retirement plan, and a good

---

[21] All historical investment and inflation statistics used in this article were obtained from Ibbotson Associates; Stocks, Bonds, Bills and Inflation, 1999 Yearbook. Ibbotson's Large Company stock data were used as a proxy for Blue Chip stocks and Ibbotson's Small Company stock data were used as a proxy for Growth stocks.

historical perspective will go a long way toward helping you make these determinations.

People need retirement strategies that will help make their assets last a long time and protect them against the ravages of inflation. This is really just another way of saying that you need to know how to manage their retirement portfolios during retirement in order to generate increasing amounts of income from year to year.[22]

---

[22] This article, "Managing Money During Retirement - A New Way to Navigate Changing Realities" by Paul A. Grangaard, is reprinted (in part) with the publisher's permission from the Journal of Retirement Planning, Vol. 3 No. 3, a bi-monthly journal published by CCH INCORPORATED. Copying or distribution without the publisher's permission is prohibited.

LONG-TERM CARE

Questions to Think About Before You Buy

In order to make the right choice in a long-term care policy, you need to answer these five questions for yourself:

1. Should you select the option for care outside as well as inside of the home?

2. What size daily benefit should be selected?

3. What elimination period should be selected?

4. What term of coverage makes sense?

5. Is a lump sum payment or annual payment policy better?

Let's address some of these selection issues. In reference to care inside versus outside of the home, many people have a preference to receive care inside of the home. While this is understandable, the more important coverage is for care outside of the home.

If your health condition deteriorates significantly, you could require care many hours each day. While a policy that pays you $100 per day would cover most of the cost for care outside of the home,[23] it may only cover one third of the care inside of the home. Let's say you needed someone to be with you around the clock. Twenty-four hours at $15 per hour is $360 per day![24] The $100 per day insurance would leave you with a huge bill to cover out of your own pocket. Therefore, never take the risk of covering care just inside of the home, since you could incur large expenses that will far exceed the coverage of your policy.

Whenever you purchase any type of insurance, always cover your worst risk first. In other words, buy insurance first for a catastrophic situation and then for the less serious risks.

Another common mistake is the selection of a 90-day elimination period. This is the period of time (commonly the first 90 days) when you must pay for long-term care from your pocket. The long-term care insurance policy would start paying on the 91st day. Many people believe that Medicare covers the first 90 days. Wrong!

Medicare can cover up to the first 100 days of a nursing home stay. But only days of skilled nursing care (not custodial or intermediate), meeting the following requirements:[25]

---

[23] A 2002 survey of 2,462 skilled and intermediate care nursing homes in all 50 states conducted by General Electric Capital Assurance Company found an average monthly cost of $4,698.
[24] 2002 Directory of California Local Area Wages CCOIS Survey. CCOIS is the California Cooperative Occupational Information System.
[25] Long-Term Care Handbook by National Underwriter.

- Following a three-day stay in a hospital.
- Admission to a nursing home within 30 days of hospital discharge.
- The nursing home must be Medicare certified.
- A physician must certify the need for skilled care on a daily basis.

All four of these requirements must be met or Medicare will not pay the claim.

Medicare's requirements are so restrictive in qualifying for "skilled" nursing care, that Medicare only pays 10% of all nursing home expenses in the U.S.[26] Forget about getting any money from Medicare, since the chances are small. If you cannot afford to cover the first 90 days out of your own pocket, then get insured for this through your long-term care policy.

Other issues regarding the selection of a long-term care policy will be covered in upcoming sections of this chapter.

You Need to Compare Policies

We know that there are 34 million seniors (age 65+) in the United States. We also know that 43% of those seniors will need some long-term care during their lifetimes.[27] Yet only 6% of seniors have long-term care protection.[28] Why is there such a disparity between those who need protection versus those who have protection?

---

[26] Healthcare Financing Administration Statistics, 2003.
[27] Technical Report 1-01, Scripps Gerontology Center, 2/01.
[28] Tillinghast, Towers Perrin "Emphasis," third quarter, 2002.

There is unnecessary confusion that exists and many seniors think that choosing the right long-term care protection is difficult and requires a lot of study.

Here's an example. A couple has a list of 15 questions about long-term care coverage. Ten of those questions were moot because, under state law, every policy must abide by those 10 issues.

Only five questions were left that needed to be answered by the client.

1. What is the length of coverage requested?

2. How much daily benefit is requested?

3. Is in-home care desired?

4. Is inflation protection desired?

5. How many deductible days (elimination period) are desired?

So, until the applicant can answer these five questions, there is no comparison among policies that cannot be accomplished. As with most financial decisions, the important questions concern your own needs and desires, not the features of the product.

Therefore, know exactly what you are after before looking at different policies from different companies. That way, you will not get overwhelmed because you will know the features that you seek.

Find a Long-Term Care Expert

Have you ever noticed that insurance companies make up difficult words for simple ideas? For instance, long-term care policies use the word "ambulating" to mean walking. Why would anyone focus on such a small matter? Because these words can mean the difference between collecting on a policy and not collecting on it. If you don't understand the fine print or get an advisor who does, you could be left out in the cold.

For example, a highly rated long-term care company agrees to pay benefits when the insured cannot perform two out of six "activities of daily living." However, their list of activities does not include ambulating (walking). This means that the insured may not be able to walk, but would also need a failure in two additional activities of daily living in order to collect benefits. Such a policy makes it difficult to collect for the insured or requires that the insured be more disabled before he or she can collect benefits.

Other policies contain features that reduce the benefits you can receive. For example, some policies require that you pay the first 90 days of care (this would be $13,500 at a hypothetical $150/day) each time you enter a period of long-term care. For someone who has two or three bouts of needing such assistance, it could cost him or her $13,500 each time he or she has a period of care.

Some policies limit the benefits paid by the day. Others set the limit by the week. The latter policy is better for the insured, particularly when home care is considered. It's possible that someone receiving home care has a need for four days per week of care that costs

$150 per day. If the policy had a $100 per day limitation, the insured is left to pay the other $50 per day for each of the four days. If instead, a policy has a limit of $600 per week, then the policy would absorb the entire cost.

What's the lesson here? You will never know everything you need to know to make the right decision about long-term care policies. You need to get advice from an expert on which policy can really be of some benefit to you. So meet with a professional who can compare these more technical features among companies for you.

Do You Have Adequate Health Insurance?

You might think your HMO is great, but it won't cover the ramifications of the following illnesses:

- Limitations of Parkinson's Disease
- Extra Care Needed to Deal with Chronic Arthritis
- Incapacity of Multiple Sclerosis
- Disability Caused by Stroke
- Care Needed Due to Alzheimer's

Your insurance and health care in the U.S. is designed to handle acute illnesses—illnesses that the doctors can fix by checking you into the hospital, fixing you and then releasing you. However, many illnesses do not behave this way. Many have a long-term debilitating nature and your insurance will not cover these long-term costs resulting from the illness.

About 6% of people over the age of 65 in the U.S. have purchased long-term care insurance to cover these costs.[29] They have realized the inadequacy of their own health insurance and pursued the protection they need. Other people close their eyes to the facts.

At $155 per day for long-term care,[30] a person can accumulate a fairly significant long-term health care bill. While many seniors would never consider being uninsured for routine health care, they are content to close their eyes to the risk that their health insurance won't cover the entire list of possible afflictions.

Get your Money Back If You Don't Use It

Imagine if you paid your homeowners insurance all of your life and never made a claim. Eventually, your insurance company sent you a check with a note that said: "Here's your money back because you never made a claim."

---

[29] Ibid.
[30] A 2002 survey of 2,462 skilled and intermediate care nursing homes in all 50 states conducted by General Electric Capital Assurance Company found an average monthly cost of $4,698.

Table 5.1
Chances of Life Risk Occurrences
and Insurance Coverage Risks

RISKS IN YOUR LIFE	ANNUAL CHANCE OF OCCURRENCE	ARE YOU INSURED?
House Burning	1 in 333	Yes
Car Crash	1 in 8	Yes
Medical Problem	Yearly?	Yes
Long-Term Health	43 in 100	NO!

Sources for Table 5.1 include: 2004 National Safety Council website; 3/31/00 National Fire Prevention Association; John Hancock website 1/14/04, http://www.gltc.jhancock.com/ltcbasics/quiz.cfm, June 2003, Fire Protection Agency, U.S. Census American Housing Survey.

Homeowners insurance companies generally don't send your money back, but there are long-term care companies that will. This practice is called "return of premium" and it refunds your premiums at death if you do not use the insurance.[31]

Being over the age of 60, you either own long-term care insurance or you have thought about getting it. You might procrastinate getting this important coverage because you may feel that your money will be wasted if you don't use the insurance (although the same holds true for your car insurance and homeowners insurance, but you would never think of not having these policies).

---

[31] Return of premium is not available on all policies and may not be available in every state.

Your solution is the return-of-premium feature. It's an optional feature offered by only a few long-term care insurance companies. With this feature, the insurance company will refund 100% of your premiums if you do not use the policy and then die.[32] You pay extra for this refund, but if you bet correctly, all of the premiums you pay will be refunded. Of course, the check will go to your beneficiary.

This is a brief summary of the return-of-premium feature. If you do not already have long-term care insurance, this may be a feature you want to add, especially if you want the coverage, but do not feel you will ever use it.

Thinking of Waiting?

In discussing financial protection for long-term care needs, some people ask why they shouldn't wait to buy a long-term care policy. After all, they argue, each year I wait, I can invest the money that would have been spent on insurance. At first this argument may make sense, but it loses its validity when asked if they do the same with their homeowners insurance.

The problem with any insurable risk is that you never know when the problem will strike. In the case of long-term care, the "problem" may not be a long-term care need. It might merely be that some condition that appears in your medical records makes you uninsurable—forever.

---

[32] One example is Life Investors Goldencare Personal Solutions Policy.

Therefore, the real risk of waiting is becoming uninsurable. In California, insurers reject one in four applicants according to the findings of the California Partnership for Long-Term Care. In many cases, the applicant is rejected simply because he or she has waited too long and his or her health records contain negative information.

As with any insurance, you have to get it when you don't need it because insurance companies do not sell insurance to people who need it (e.g. try to buy homeowners insurance while your house is burning down).

The chance of becoming uninsurable aside, does it make financial sense to wait? At age 60, if a package of benefits costs about $1,200, at age 70, you can expect to pay about $2,500 for the same policy (Weinstein, 1998; GE Financial Network, 2001). The risk of becoming uninsurable also increases with age.

Table 5.2
Cost of Waiting until Age 65
to Get Long-Term Care Insurance

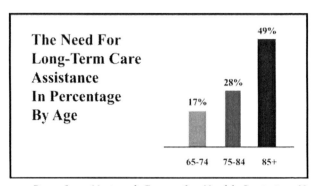

Source: Data from National Center for Health Statistics, Health Interview Survey.

Tax Break?

The federal government decided it could not afford to finance long-term care coverage for seniors. So, it announced that by giving a tax break, it would assist seniors to buy their own long-term care insurance. But let's take a close look, and we'll see this "tax break" is more rhetoric than substance. In fact, by pursuing this tax break, you could be much worse off.

Here's what the government offered. The tax law allows anyone who buys a "qualified" long-term care policy to deduct the premium. In addition, the government promises that when you receive benefits from the policy, the benefits will be non-taxable. At first glance, it looks like you win on both ends with the qualified long-term care policy. However, there are limits to the deduction. The long-term care premium must be added to your regular medical expenses, and you can deduct the total amount that exceeds 7.5% of your income.[33]

Here's an example. Let's say you have an income of $40,000. Since you belong to an HMO, you have no medical expenses other than a hypothetical $500 in non-covered prescriptions. You pay a hypothetical $2,000 annually for your qualified long-term care policy. So the total of your premium and medical expenses is $2,500 or 6.25% of your income. Since the total is less than 7.5% of your income, you cannot deduct your premium. In this case, the government's gift is worthless and it is just rhetoric.

---

[33] IRS Publication 17, 2003.

But what about the fact that you get the benefits from the policy tax free? Isn't that a major benefit of qualified policies? Maybe not. Up until 1997, benefits from any long-term care policy were tax free, and the government has remained silent on the following question: "Aren't the benefits from a qualified or non-qualified policy tax free anyway?" Many accountants advise their clients that since the government never changed the old law, benefits from any long-term care policy are tax free, just like disability benefits.

Other accountants point out another issue which should keep the benefits from being largely tax free. If you collect $40,000 in benefits to pay for the cost of a nursing care, you will deduct $40,000 that year in medical expenses. The two items will mostly cancel each other out, making most of your policy benefits untaxed.

So why would anyone buy a qualified long-term care policy, given the fact that the benefits are less than non-qualified, as well as harder to obtain than the regular non-qualified policy? (Because qualified policies leave out ambulating as a trigger to collect benefits.) Check with a qualified tax advisor or financial advisor before making such a purchase.

Is the Company Healthy?

Occasionally, people interested in long-term care will express their concern about the uncertainty of being able to actually collect benefits from the insurance company when they need it. This is a valid concern. People don't generally have difficulty getting paid by long-term care insurers, but your advisor should check with the Department of Insurance regularly to ensure that the companies dealt with have no outstanding violations.

But the real key to making sure you can collect is to select a long-term care insurance company with liberal claim policies. One insurer has instituted the most liberal policies available. Most long-term care policies pay benefits based on one of two conditions: either you have disability in performing two activities of daily living (i.e. bathing, dressing, ambulating, eating, toileting, continence, transferring) or cognitive impairment (i.e. dementia).

One insurance company (and maybe others), however, provides yet two more ways to collect benefits.[34]

1. If your doctor determines that nursing care is a medical necessity. The insurance company will accept the determination of your own family physician.

2. The company will pay home care benefits (if you select home care coverage) if you have problems performing two or more "instrumental" activities of daily living. These instrumental activities include: cooking, shopping, housekeeping, laundry, bill paying, telephoning, and medication management.

If you want to make the right choice in selecting long-term care coverage, understand that all policies are

---

[34] Penn Treaty Comprehensive Policy PF2600, 1/04.

not alike. They may look alike and have similar prices, but when it comes to collecting benefits, you want a policy that has liberal features.

Asset Protection Plan

What if you could buy insurance under the following terms?

- You pay a single premium (rather than pay annual premiums).
- That premium earns interest that accrues to your benefit.
- If you never use the insurance, then you can take the premium back, plus interest.
- If you die with the insurance, then your beneficiaries receive more than you deposited.
- If you need the insurance, then the premium you paid purchases you a substantial benefit to cover your expenses.

In other words, if you don't need the insurance, you get back at least the amount you paid. If you do need the insurance, it's there for you.

This is called a "linked benefit policy."[35] Thousands of seniors are using it to obtain coverage for long-term care, knowing that if they don't use the insurance, the premium can be withdrawn by them or the policy will pay off to their heirs as a tax-free death benefit. Heads you win, tails you win!

---

[35] Such policies offered by First Penn Pacific, Lincoln Benefit Life, Golden Care, and possibly others.

If you'd like to see an illustration for your own situation and you do not already have long-term care coverage, contact a long-term care professional to obtain an illustration.

What are You Waiting On?

A gentleman who recently obtained long-term care insurance hesitated between the first and second meeting with his advisor, stating that he had spoken with several of his friends and none of them had obtained this protection. He questioned whether he needed it. This gentleman was a successful businessman and an astute thinker. The advisor explained to him, "It's not you who is overlooking something; it is they who are ignoring a serious issue."

Unfortunately, many investors feel best about a financial move when everyone else is making the same move. In our culture, we have a saying, "There is safety in numbers." However, lynch mobs, radical groups, and sub-culture factions are also "numbers" of people banding together to create chaos and bedlam. Unfortunately, there can often be ignorance and foolishness in numbers.

Whether others are acting to protect themselves does not alter the facts:[36]

- 43 of every 100 people age 65 or over will have a need for long-term care assistance, either in the home or a facility outside of the home.

[36] Technical Report 1-01, Scripps Gerontology Center, 2/01.

- 83% of these cases will be serious—requiring care of four months or longer.

Compare the chance of this risk to the chance that your home will burn down or that your car will be totaled. Despite the odds, you would never think of leaving these risks uninsured. If you are over the age of 65 and have not investigated your options for handling the risks of long-term care, please contact me or call for a free copy of The Long-Term Care Buyers Guide.

You Don't Want to Go on Medicaid

In a business that helps seniors with financial matters, the issue of preparing for long-term care needs always comes up. Sometimes, the response is, "I'll just go on Medicaid."

While the government set up the Medicaid system to support destitute people as their last resort, there is a good reason you do not want to go on Medicaid. Let me explain by first sharing a quote from the California Advocates for Nursing Home Reform:

> "While spending down is easy to do and to document, it may be difficult to find a nursing home placement if you have no resources and must find a bed in a Medicaid-certified facility. The longer you pay as a private patient, the more options you have when looking for a nursing home. In most areas, Medicaid pays less per day than the amount a facility will charge a private pay resident...In some cases, even though Medicaid discrimination is illegal, facilities

are unwilling to accept residents who are eligible for Medicaid upon admission."

We have also heard many stories of discrimination against Medicaid residents with a lower standard of care. For example, if a nursing home routinely charges $4,000 a month to provide a nice sunny private room to a private-pay patient, do you think they will provide the same when they are only receiving $3,000 per month for a Medicaid resident?

Michael McDermott, a Maryland health care consultant describes the issue:

> "When the mayor of a city walks into a restaurant, there's no policy that dictates he or she will get the best table, the thickest steak and superior service at the expense of other patrons. But that's what often happens. The same thing is occurring in nursing homes. Any nursing home operator will pick a private-pay patient over a Medicaid [patient]. This attitude filters down to the staff and it affects Medicaid patients' quality of life on a day-to-day basis."[37]

If you want quality care for yourself or your family members, do not depend on government support for it; instead, be prepared to pay for it. At least be prepared to pay for three years of care from your own pocket (or from an insurance policy) to help obtain placement in a quality location. Additionally, while Medicaid will not provide long-term care in the home, with your own funds or private insurance, you can be covered to provide care in your own home.

[37] Kiplinger Retirement Report, 4/00.

Let's hope you never have to face this issue, but the only way to avoid catastrophes in life is to be prepared or insured for them. Remember, the chance of your house burning down is 1 in 333.[38] The chance of you needing some long-term care if over age 65 is almost 5 in 10.[39] If you have your house insured, then why isn't your health insured?

How to Reduce the Cost

You may find that long-term care salespeople want to sell you the most expensive policy. While we believe that you should have complete coverage (inflation protection, lifetime coverage, at least $100/day benefit), it is better to have at least a basic policy than to have none at all. In other words, a minimum policy is better than being uncovered for the high cost of long-term care. In order to help you minimize the cost of insurance, we have compiled these five ways to help you reduce costs and yet provide basic coverage. None of us know when a health catastrophe can strike. An onset of a heart attack, stroke, cancer, Parkinson's, and Alzheimer's are debilitating illnesses, which give no advance warning. Protect yourself and your family financially.

Here are five ways to get covered at a lower cost:

1. **Reduce the coverage period.** For example, reduce the term of the policy from four years to three years. Savings can still be

---

[38] National Fire Prevention Association, 3/31/00.
[39] John Hancock website on Long-Term Care, www.gltc.jhancock.com/ltcbasics/quiz.cfm.

significant and a three-year policy covers 72% of the cases of long-term care.[40]

2. **Reduce the daily benefit.** The actual cost of nursing care averages $155/day.[41] If you cover just $100 or $90 per day with insurance, some people can make up the difference with other income sources, such as Social Security or interest income.[42]

3. **If you are age 75 or over,** consider omitting the inflation protection. Although you will hopefully never need long-term care, if you do, you are likely to need it within 10 years—by age 85. Therefore, you do not need to protect for inflation over as long a period of time as, for example, a 65-year-old would need to prepare.

4. **Consider partial home care coverage.** Many companies offer, as an example, $100/day benefit for nursing home payments and $50/day for home care payments (home care costs can be less expensive if you have

---

[40] Twenty-eight percent of people required a nursing home stay of more than three years, Technical Report 1-01, Scripps Gerontology Center, 2/01.

[41] A 2002 survey of 2,462 skilled and intermediate care nursing homes in all 50 states conducted by General Electric Capital Assurance Company found an average daily rate of approximately $155/day.

[42] If you have sufficient interest income or Social Security income, it may be better for you to insure for a majority of the cost of long-term care and self-insure for the remainder. This has the effect of lowering the current cost of the insurance premiums without subjecting you to being unable to cover the costs of long-term care, if and when they arise.

family or friends who can help with care).
By reducing the benefits for home care, you
can lower your premium.

5. **Eliminate home care insurance.** Many
   people have a spouse or friends or relatives
   who can assist them in the home. Hired
   home aides are relatively inexpensive
   ($18.12 per hour).[43] Care at home may
   easily be covered within the means of your
   own income. The most important coverage
   to obtain is for care outside of the home.

Have an experienced agent shop around many
companies to find you the best coverage for your
budget.

---

[43] 2002 Directory of California Local Area Wages for wages from
the 1999-2001 CCOIS Survey. CCOIS is the California
Cooperative Occupational Information System.

ESTATE PLANNING

Please Note: *Nothing herein is intended to serve as legal advice. These articles simply address educational issues about estate planning. Consult an attorney when dealing with these issues.*

Avoid Probate Without An Expensive Trust

Until recently, the best advice for avoiding probate for many people was to obtain a living trust. That's because most assets must be probated even though you have a will. The exception to this has always been IRAs, annuities and bank accounts with a "pay on death" designation. It has not been possible to avoid probate on stocks, bonds and mutual funds without a living trust—until now.

The California legislature has enacted the "Transfer on Death" provision. It allows you to have stocks, bonds and other securities pass directly to your beneficiary without probate and without a need for a living trust.

How to you take advantage of this? Your mutual fund company or brokerage firm should have a form for you to complete. If you keep your investments spread all over, you will need to complete a form for each institution. Better yet, we can help you consolidate all your assets into one account and then you need just one form to cover all securities.

So if you have a simple estate, the Transfer on Death form could preclude the need for a living trust. (Please consult an attorney as we are not attorneys nor do we practice law).

How People Mess Up Their Living Trust

Many people do the right thing by having a living trust prepared. After all, why would anyone subject his or her heirs to a lengthy, costly and needless probate process? However, these same trustees fail to investigate how to make the most of the trust and feel that the "job is done" once they have their trust completed. In fact, many people make enormous errors, which can be extremely costly.

> **Error #1: Leaving assets outright to heirs.** Some trusts leave assets outright to heirs, which means that the heirs are free to squander the assets and the heirs' creditors are free to attach these assets. In other words, many people have instructions in their trusts that when they die, the assets are distributed to the heirs outright. Wouldn't it make more sense to leave assets to heirs in trust so that they will be protected from outside forces and so that the trustee can also control the squandering of the assets? Additionally, by leaving assets in a trust,

they can be kept out of the heirs' estates, so as to avoid estate taxes again. It's an often observed phenomena that the next generation dissipates the wealth created by the parents. The parents are sometimes contributors by leaving the assets to heirs outright.

One suggestion would be a simple process whereby your living trust has assets placed in a bypass trust at your death. That bypass trust continues indefinitely, for the entire lives of your children (and can even continue for additional generations). The income from the trust can be distributed to your heirs and you can leave precise instructions for when and how the principal can be distributed (e.g. to buy a house, to start a business or at age 60, etc.). While assets remain in this bypass trust, they enjoy protection from creditors and also family disputes. Your son or daughter may have a great marriage today, but if divorce occurs and the assets you have left get commingled, your son-in-law or daughter-in-law may have a claim to these assets. If the assets are in trust, no claim can be exercised.

Error #2: Failure to manage the bypass trust correctly. When one spouse dies, a bypass trust is created and funded with assets of the deceased spouse. Many people do not think about which assets to place in the bypass trust and how they should be managed. Selecting the right assets is very important for tax reasons and wealth creation. Assets in the bypass trust should have two objectives—(1) grow as much as possible and (2) generate no taxes. In fact,

these assets are often managed incorrectly
most of the time in the following way.

The surviving spouse invests the bypass assets to
generate income for his or her own benefit. At the same
time, his or her own assets are growing in value (e.g.
stocks and house) and become subject to estate taxes.
This makes no sense. In fact, the surviving spouse
should spend down his or her own assets to ensure that
those assets will be below the estate taxable level
(indicated on the chart following this section), while
allowing the assets in the bypass trust to grow as much
as possible. Many people do just the opposite with the
assets in order to minimize tax and maximize wealth
creation.

In fact, one of the best uses of a bypass trust is to
use it as an irrevocable life insurance trust. Such an
arrangement can pay off several times to the heirs,
through completely tax-free life insurance benefits. In
this case, some or all of the assets in the bypass trust are
used to purchase a life insurance policy for the heirs'
benefit. When the second parent dies, the life insurance
pays off, providing a potentially large payment to the
heirs. This payment is free of estate and income taxes.
Depending on the parent's age and health when the
insurance policy is obtained, the proceeds to heirs could
realistically be 200% to 600% of the premium invested.

**Error #3: Selecting the wrong successor
trustee.** Many parents select one or all of
their children as successor trustee(s). This
can be a formula for disaster and create
hard feelings among siblings,
misunderstandings and even costly mistakes

if the children do not have business savvy. People should be encouraged to select an independent trustee who is knowledgeable in estate matters and can settle an estate efficiently. A trustworthy attorney, accountant, or financial advisor is usually a good choice.

Table 6.1
Scheduled Estate Tax Exemption
per Person as of 1/29/04

Year	Amount
2004	$1,500,000
2005	$1,500,000
2006	$2,000,000
2007	$2,000,000
2008	$2,000,000
2009	$3,500,000

Reminder: Congress can change the above figures at any time.

The Second Half of the Game

Investors want to know the best place to invest money. Unfortunately, the investor is often focused on the wrong part of his or her financial situation. Does it really matter if an investor can get a 12% return rather than 6%, if he or she ignores his or her estate planning situation and pays the government an unnecessary $500,000? Wouldn't it make more sense for an investor to focus on the best way to save that $500,000 rather than focusing on how to invest $50,000 to earn another $3,000 per year? The answer is obvious, but it's not how many people behave.

Why do investors behave in this way? Most investors incorrectly believe that estate planning is about giving money away and losing control over their assets. This mistaken perception is promoted by attorneys and advisors who provide shallow advice about simplistic strategies of gifting money away or giving it to charity.

For example, a common recommendation is to place money in an irrevocable trust in order to remove it from your estate. That common suggestion means you lose control. If these advisors really kept current with their field, they would also know that money can be made exempt from estate taxes, while still giving you access to the funds. You do not need to lose control. In other words, assets can indeed be placed in an irrevocable trust, which removes them from your estate and from estate taxes. That same trust can also contain provisions for providing distributions to your spouse, if your spouse needs them, or loans back to you if you need the assets.

If you listen to many advisors, it sounds like estate planning is about relinquishing control of your assets. When in fact, estate planning is about maintaining control of your assets. Just look what happens if you do not utilize estate planning—the government takes control over your money and here's how they spend your estate taxes:[44]

---

[44] IRS Form 1040 Instruction Booklet, 2003.

- Defense (20%)
- Interest on National Debt (8%)
- Physical and Community Development (10%)
- Social Programs (21%)
- Law Enforcement (3%)
- Social Security, Medicare & Other Retirement (38%)

If you don't like how the government spends your money, estate planning will redirect how your money is spent, based on your desires. Therefore, estate planning is about taking maximum control of your money to be directed based on your desires, not the government's desires.

Other reasons that investors fail to do estate planning include just plain ignorance or mistakes in their knowledge. Some investors still think that if they have a living trust, they'll pay no estate taxes. This is a widely held misconception.

Other investors hate talking about estate planning because they'll have to confront mortality. And as mentioned before, some investors think that estate planning means giving money away. In fact, good estate planning starts with making sure you have ample resources for yourself. Good estate planning provides that you pay less income taxes today, you have increased income, and you can possibly liquidate assets without capital gains tax. Estate planning is for you, as well as the next generation

Regarding estate taxes, some think their estate planning problem will go away because the government is raising the level on the estate tax exemption (the exemption is equal to $1.5 million per person in 2004, rising to $3.5 million in 2009). Don't forget, however, that the government giveth and taketh and the next congress could easily lower the exemption. Since dead people don't vote, the estate tax is the easiest tax to levy.

Estate planning boils down to one simple issue—do you want to have control of your money? How do you start? One way is to start by having clients complete a questionnaire that helps them focus on their goals and desires. The questionnaire is followed up with an interview to help translate the answers into specific desires. Only then do we go to work to determine ways to achieve what our client wants. This avoids the mistake that many make, by jumping right into the tools (trusts, gifting, insurance), only to learn later that the tools don't work as desired.

So if you really want to make a big difference in your financial picture, it may make more sense to focus on estate planning rather than on how to get a higher percentage on your investments (a percentage that the government may get most of anyway).

Taxes on Annuities

Lots of seniors have purchased fixed annuities for their safety, simplicity and income tax deferral. Yet some annuity owners lose half of their annuity value and most aren't even aware of this! Let's look at how this happens with a hypothetical example.

When Mary was 60, she purchased a fixed annuity for $50,000. She held it for 10 years and the interest accumulated nicely. The account doubled to $100,000 (a compound rate of 7.17% which could have been locked in 10 years ago per data from *Annuity Shopper Magazine,* Dec. 2001). So far, Mary was very happy with this safe alternative. She never gave much thought to what happens to the annuity at her death. She figured she would eventually withdraw the money and use it.

The truth is, fewer than 30% of the annuity owners make any withdrawals from their annuity.[45] If the owner passes away, the policies can get hit with some very large taxes.

Annuity Value	$100,000
Income Tax	-16,500
Estate Tax	-40,800[46]
Beneficiaries get	$ 42,700

Note that estate taxes are paid by people with estates of over $1.5 million, which would apply to Mary in the previous example. In Mary's case, that's the picture at the time of death when the taxes are due.

In the blink of an eye, Mary's beneficiary loses $57,300—over half of the annuity value! Is there a remedy? YES!

If you do not plan to use the annuity for yourself, you can make a smart move with the following tactic:

---

[45] Gallup Organization Survey of Annuity Owners, 2001.
[46] This analysis may not be accurate for every annuity owner as single people with estates less than 1.5 million (in 2004 and 2005) do not pay estate taxes. We assume a federal and state **combined** income tax bracket of 33% which may be higher or lower than your actual tax bracket. A single taxpayer with taxable income over $68,800 will have a federal income tax bracket of 28% (for 2004) and a 5% state tax bracket in high tax states such as California. Estate taxes are assumed at 48%.

Annuitize the annuity (deferred taxes or sales charges could apply or 10% tax penalty if under age 59½—please call for a review of your contract). When you annuitize the annuity, you select a payout option that may include a lifetime income from the annuity company. You trade the $100,000 balance for a guaranteed income for life (or any period you choose). (The shorter the period, the higher will be the monthly income paid to you.)

Mary had her insurance company make monthly payments to her of $655.[47] She did not need the money, so she used the after tax amount to purchase a life insurance policy (fixed universal life policy) on her life, payable to her beneficiaries. (Fixed universal life policies may include substantial fees, charges, expenses, and tax consequences.) Based on Mary's current age of 70 (and assuming she is a preferred nonsmoker female), this $655 ($508 after taxes) per month purchased her a universal life policy with a death benefit of $231,664.[48]

---

[47] This is an average of immediate annuity payments from the top 40 annuity companies as reported by Comparative Annuity Reports as of 1/04, female, age 70, lifetime monthly payments. The average monthly payments are comprised of principal and interest. The exclusion percentage is 42% (per IRS as of 2004). Therefore, 68% of the $655 monthly would be taxable at an assumed tax rate of 33% (28% federal plus 5% state). Tax calculates to $147 leaving Mary $508 after taxes.

[48] Premiums would be higher for smokers and/or those not qualifying for preferred rates. Transamerica Occidental Life TransACE EX, Form 1-12006102 (fixed UL) for a female 70-year-old preferred nonsmoker provides a guaranteed death benefit of $231,664 to age 100 as of 1/19/04. Guarantee based on the claims-paying ability of the insurance company.

Now, instead of Mary's heirs getting only $42,700 at her death (the amount that they would have received after the taxes on the annuity), the heirs receive $231,664 of life insurance death benefit, free of estate and income tax![49] That's over five times as much money for the beneficiaries, over $188,000 more!

Let's say Mary started the payments from the annuity. For each payment she receives from the annuity, she is paying for the life insurance. Even if she died after the first premium on the life insurance, her beneficiaries would still receive the entire $231,664 death benefit on the life insurance policy.

$27 Billion in Estate Taxes in 2002[50]

The annual report on the United States Government reports that Americans paid $27 billion in estate taxes. Every dime of those taxes could have been avoided. How do you think the children felt when they wrote out a check for $300,000 for estate taxes and then learned from the attorney that their parents could have saved them every penny?

If you don't like wasting money on taxes and don't want your kids squandering money either, then this section will explain what you need to do. First, you must realistically answer the following questions.

---

[49] We can explain the additional estate planning required to keep the proceeds of your life insurance policy out of your estate so that it passes **free of estate taxes**. Additionally, you need to qualify medically and financially for the life insurance coverage. This suggestion may not be beneficial in all cases. It depends on your income and estate tax bracket.

[50] IRS revenue by type of tax, www.irs.gov/pub/irs-soi/02db07co.xls.

- Will your estate be worth more than the current exemption amount when you die? By the way, you cannot assume that the estate exemption will be held indefinitely at the anticipated levels, as some people believe. Many people do not realize that the act "sunsets" or expires at the end of 2010. This means that individuals that live at least to the end of the decade may very well not receive anything close to the anticipated exemption.

- Do you have any assets that could be double taxed at your death (double taxed by income and estate taxes, which could consume almost 70% of the value) such as IRAs and annuities?[51]

- Do you think that if you need to take action, your attorney will call you up on the phone and tell you? (He or she may not, since many attorneys wait until you call them.)

- Do you think you have plenty of time to take care of any estate tax problem—like the people who paid $27 billion in 2002?

- Do you incorrectly think that estate planning means giving up control of assets or making gifts or giving to charity? (With good estate planning, you can exercise control of your assets and still remove them from your taxable estate.)

- Do you have the false notion that a living trust will eliminate your estate taxes? (In 2004 and

---

[51] Income tax of 35% and estate tax of 48% after credit for IRD.

2005, you will pay estate taxes on assets over $1.5 million, living trust or not.)

- Do you think that you need to die in order to get your current exemption amount? (Well, you don't. It's available right now and many wealthy people use their exemptions when they can make the most of them—during their lifetimes.)

If you answered "yes" to any of the above questions, then you probably have an estate tax problem. It's time to see a professional.

A Common Mistake

Many spouses hold property as joint tenants. Generally, that's a bad idea and here's why. If you and your spouse hold assets as **community property**, when one spouse dies, the other spouse can sell the property without taxes (all prior capital gains are erased). However, if the property is held as joint tenants, the deceased party has the capital gains erased on his or her half, but the capital gains tax is due on the other half that is sold by the surviving spouse. Therefore, in order to eliminate all capital gains tax, you need to hold appreciating assets with your spouse as community property.

You can easily change the title on your assets. For your house, you can usually get the right form at your county recorder's office or a nearby title company. For securities, simply notify your brokerage firm that you desire a change and they will open a new account with the right title.

What about joint tenancy with your kids? It's a bad idea. If your son is in a car accident and gets sued, then the plaintiff can come after the assets you hold jointly with your son and force the sale of that asset.

Simple estate planning mistakes can have BIG costs. The following basic rules serve most people well. Avoid probate by using a living trust, not by titling assets in joint tenancy. If a living trust is not used, a husband and wife should hold appreciating assets as community property. If a living trust is not used, some states allow probate to be avoided by placing a beneficiary name on securities and real estate. Check with your title company and securities firm.

Want to Help Your Grandchildren

Ever worry about how your grandchildren will turn out? While you can't control their future, you can be a big influence. Do you want them to get a good education? What if you told them there's $50,000 waiting for each of them if they finish college? You do not even need to be around to control this. All you have to do is set up an irrevocable trust, a gift of $11,000 annually (or $22,000 if you are married) into the trust, follow the rules for maintaining it and give your grandchildren incentive to do the right things.

In your trust, you can make up any rules you want. For example, the money can be distributed at a certain age, the money can be distributed only if the grandchild graduates with at least a "B" average, the money cannot be distributed if the grandchild ever gets involved with drugs, or the money can be distributed for the purchase of a house.

In order for the IRS to count the $11,000 gift as an exempt gift, you will need to give the beneficiaries a limited annual right of withdrawal (called "Crummey Powers"). However, you can also make it clear, in an informal way, that if the beneficiaries exercise their Crummey power, you will stop making the annual gifts. In this manner, the fund will build up in the trust to be distributed based on your wishes.

Can you gift more to the grandchildren if you desire? Yes, but the IRS has a special tax called the "Generation Skipping Transfer" tax. The IRS has this in place because they attempt to collect taxes at every generation. However, if you give gifts that skip generations, then the IRS could lose out on estate tax revenues. Thus, you are limited to gifts of $1.1 million (per spouse) to grandchildren without an additional tax being levied.

Whether your gifts are large or small, you can't control the future, but you can definitely influence it. With all generations, money talks.

Compass™ Snapshot Tells You If You Should Be Concerned

Everyone who defines themselves as "middle income" or higher should be concerned about estate taxes. For every penny you have over the current exemption amount at death, the government will tax your estate (starting at 41%, rising to 48% as your estate gets larger).

With a rising stock market and rising home values, more people are exceeding the amount of their exemption every day. If you are only slightly above this threshold (e.g. you have an estate of $1.6 million in 2004), then it's easy to gift the excess (subject to IRS limits) to your beneficiaries now and avoid the estate taxes. **By the way, a living trust does not avoid estate taxes.**

If you are substantially over this amount, your estate is probably growing faster than your gifts will reduce your estate (non-taxable gifts are limited to $11,000 per year, per recipient). So how do you avoid estate taxes?

Rather than waiting to use your exemption, you can use it now. For example, let's say you have an amount of stock today that is equal in value to the current exemption amount ($1.5 million in 2004-2005) that you plan on leaving to your estate. If you gift it today, you can use your exemption and give it away tax free. If you wait, the stock could double in value over the next ten years and then you have an even bigger estate tax problem. Below is a comparison.

Table 6.2
Estate Taxes for Inclusion or Removal of
Stock from an Estate

	Inside Your Estate	Removed From Your Estate
Value of Stock Today	$1,500,000	$1,500,000
Value of Stock in 10 Years (7.9% Annual Growth)	$3,204,225	$3,204,225
Estate Tax (At Today's Rates)	$803,028	-0-

You may be reluctant to give up control of the stock through a gift and you do not need to give up control. The gift can be made in the form of a trust, which you or your spouse can tap into if needed, or you can continue to control the stock through a family limited partnership and continue to receive income (in the form of management fees or loans).

Still Supporting Your Children

Some parents retire, yet still support their children financially. While this is not a particularly good idea (read a copy of *The Millionaire Next Door* by Dr. Tom Stanley), it's particularly sad when parents are taking money out of their cash flow and decreasing their lifestyle, just to help their son make his mortgage payment. Here's a better way to help the kids and not get pinched in the pocketbook.

Rather than taking the money out of your cash flow, you can turn a low-yielding asset into income. For example, the average stock in the S&P 500 only pays a 1.75% dividend (*Barron's*, January 5, 2004). So, many stocks do not produce a large current income. Do you have raw land that pays you nothing? These assets can be converted into extra current income that can be used to help your children. Are you worried about the capital gains? Here's how to beat that.

A "Capital Gains Elimination Trust" (10% of the money must be left to charity, so this is often called a "Charitable Remainder Trust") allows you to sell the asset (stocks, real estate, etc.), pay no capital gains tax, reinvest the proceeds for higher income, and receive that income. How much income can you receive? As long as the calculations indicate that 10% of the balance will remain for charity, the income and the original capital can all be paid out over time to yourselves or your children. By using this method, you don't need to cut into your regular cash flow in order to help your children.

Let's take an example. Mary and David (parents) own stock worth $1 million. The dividends are only 1.25% annually or $12,500. They desire to have more income, but have kept the stock because the capital gains taxes would be high. Here's the solution:

1. Have an attorney draw up a "Capital Gains Elimination Trust."

2. Contribute the stock to the trust.

3. The trust sells the stock. Because the trust does not pay taxes, there is no capital gains tax due. Now, the entire $1 million can be reinvested for higher income. Let's assume the parents select fixed income instruments paying a hypothetical 8%. Their income is now $80,000 annually. That's a $67,500 increase in income from the $12,500 that they were receiving as dividends previously. (Depending on the parents' ages and interest rates, the IRS tables may allow distributions of the principal also, so that the parents could receive more than $80,000 annually.)

4. Because part of the funds will eventually pass to charity, the parents receive an income tax deduction, which is used to lower their income tax.

5. Because the $1 million of stock has been removed from their estate, their estate tax drops by over $400,000 (assuming their other assets use up the maximum exemption).

As you can see, the parents come out ahead on several fronts. Only the beneficiary would complain, because he or she would have received the $1 million in stock, less approximately $400,000 in estate tax, or $600,000. Here's the solution for that. The parents can use part of their $67,500 of extra income to buy a survivorship life insurance policy for $600,000. When they pass away, the beneficiary receives the $600,000 from the life insurance that replaces what they would have had from the stock. Now everybody is happy courtesy of the IRS.

No Game Plan

Among estate planners, Stephen Leimberg is considered a foremost expert. He is a JD, CLU, and professor of Taxation and Estate Planning at the American College in Bryn Mawr, PA. He is an attorney, nationally-known speaker and best-selling author of more than 40 books on estate, financial, and retirement planning.

Over 40,000 attorneys and estate planners subscribe to his newsletter. Here's a quotation from his article on "The Ten Most Common Estate Planning Mistakes:"

> "Mistake 10: Lack of a "Master Strategy" Game Plan. Do-it-yourself estate and financial planning is the closest thing to do-it-yourself brain surgery. Few people can

do it successfully…A key principle in estate planning is that you can't eliminate the big mistakes in your estate plan until you've identified them."

Many people think that they have done the right thing, but mistakes are common. Here is one of the most common mistakes—appointing your children to act as your executor or trustee.

In an article by Stephen Leimberg and Charles Plotnick, "Selection of Executor, Trustee and Attorney" they say that you should consider many aspects in selecting a trustee, among them:

- Availability
- Impartiality and lack of conflict of interest
- Financial security
- Investment sophistication, policy, and track record
- Business sophistication
- Accounting and tax-planning expertise
- Record-keeping and reporting ability
- Decision-making abilities
- Competence
- Integrity
- Flexibility to meet changing circumstances
- Experience as a trustee

I still hear many stories about parents who are supporting their children financially, yet have selected their children as trustees of their trust. Does a grown adult child who needs financial help meet the above standards?

If you have done nothing more than had an attorney draw up a living trust, this is hardly estate planning. You or your heirs could still be exposed to estate taxes, unnecessary income taxes, improper distribution, and liquidity problems in settling your estate. The best thing you can do is select a knowledgeable trustee to handle the trust when you are gone.

Is a Dynasty Trust Right for You?

Have you ever heard that when a family accumulates wealth, by the second generation, thereafter it's gone? A dynasty trust may help protect family wealth against several outside forces. Here's how a dynasty trust works differently than your living trust.

With your living trust, when you die, your assets are distributed to your heirs. From that moment forward, those assets are subject to eroding forces in the estates of your heirs:

- Assets are subject to claims of creditors.
- Assets can be split up in a divorce.
- Upon the death of your son or daughter, assets can be left to his or her spouse and leave your bloodline (there's no assurance the assets will reach your grandchildren).
- Assets are taxed by the IRS (possibly additional estate taxes).

If you make a small change to your living trust, you can avoid these eroding influences. Rather than leave your assets to your heirs, leave the assets in your dynasty trust. Because the assets are in trust, your heirs do not legally own them (even though you can give your heirs high accessibility or you can limit accessibility if you choose). Therefore, your heirs' creditors can't touch the assets and neither can their spouses. Unspent assets can pass from generation to generation, free of additional estate tax (limited to $1 million estate tax exemption per generation per donee). You gain assurance that assets stay in your bloodline if unspent and pass to your grandchildren.

So if you want to have your inheritance exposed to eroding forces, just leave your inheritance outright to your heirs. If, instead, you want to protect your inheritance, you can do so. The dynasty trust is just one idea that can reduce taxes and preserve wealth.

The Most Important Part of Estate Planning

Advance directives are your formal instructions in the case of your being unable to provide instructions (because of disability or illness). These are important for people of any age, so please tell your children to take care of this important business. As you should, also.

First, you should arrange for the durable power of attorney. This document gives another person the power to act on your behalf when you cannot. You can make it as broad or limited as you desire. While many people have an attorney prepare this document, many can find a sufficient pre-printed, state-approved form in a good stationery store to do the job. You select a trustworthy person (typically a family member) who can execute your affairs—pay bills, sell property, and transact business on your behalf. Without such a document, your bank or securities firm or the title company will not accept any instructions from your family on your behalf. In fact, the family would need to go to court and receive a ruling to act in your behalf. This can be an expensive, slow and unnecessary process.

The other most common document is the health care power of attorney, which empowers another person to make medical decisions when you cannot. For example, someone may need to decide which procedure would be best in discussion with your doctor or whether a certain operation should be performed. Do not confuse this with a living will, which is a document normally used to communicate your specific instructions regarding life-sustaining measures.

As you can see, having these documents prepared and others delegated to assist you is critical. These documents must be prepared in advance and any responsible adult of any age can have these in force.

Do You Still Need That Old Life Insurance Policy?

Sometimes, people find that they own life insurance policies they no longer need. The policy was purchased when they needed protection for minor children or to pay off a mortgage. In retirement, they may no longer have a need for the policy. If you are in a similar situation, what should you do with the old policy? There are several good options.[52]

1.   You could do a tax-free exchange into a "combo policy," which provides life insurance protection, plus long-term care insurance. You can simply move the cash value from your current policy to one of the new "combo policies" and pick up long-term care insurance, which should be important for retirees. There would be no cost (unless you wanted to increase the size of the policy) and you get a new, important benefit.

2.   You could surrender the policy for its cash value. Be careful, this could be a taxable event. Any cash you receive in excess of premiums paid is taxable.

3.   You could sell the policy. In some cases, you can sell the policy for more than the surrender value. This is called a "senior settlement." Here's how it works. A life insurance agent gets bids for your policy. The person who buys it keeps it. Often, they will buy it for more than the surrender value. Why? Because they are taking an investment risk. They calculate that if they keep the policy until you pass away (and they even pay premiums on it if necessary) they will make a profit when they collect

---

[52] Exchanging to a new policy could incur fees, expenses, commissions, and surrender charges. Tax-free exchanges must adhere to rules of Section 1035 of the Internal Revenue Code.

the proceeds. The amount you can sell the policy for is higher, the worse your health profile. Whether time proves if they make a good investment or not is no matter to you, as you get paid up front for the sale of the policy.

4. You could leverage the cash value for a higher death benefit. Often, older policies provided a low amount of insurance compared to the cash value. In many cases, you can exchange this old policy (at no cost or tax to you) for a new policy that has a much larger death benefit. If you like the idea of having a policy for your heirs, this may be the best option.

Do You Own a Life Insurance Policy?

Do you own a life insurance policy? It's not a good idea. It's fine to have life insurance to protect your family or for payment of estate taxes, but you never want to own it. Your life insurance policy should be owned outside of your estate. Here's why.

Your life policy has a surrender value (the amount you get if you cash it in) and a death benefit (the amount the beneficiary gets when you die). Even though the surrender value is the real value to you, the IRS will levy estate tax on the entire death benefit if this policy remains in your name (in your estate).

Let's take a step back. A life insurance policy has three parties:

- ***The Owner***—the person who controls the policy and has legal ownership.
- ***The Insured***—the person whose life is insured.
- ***The Beneficiary***—the party who gets the death benefit when the insured dies.

Many people automatically have the same party as the owner and the insured. This can be a costly mistake. In a typical situation, it would be best to have the parties set as follows:

- ***The Owner***—the children or irrevocable life insurance trust.
- ***The Insured***—you.
- ***The Beneficiary***—the children or irrevocable life insurance trust.

By setting the parties as stated, at your passing, the policy is not in your estate and will not be subject to estate taxes.

How do you get a policy out of your estate? You could gift it to your children or to an irrevocable trust that you establish for the benefit of your children. If the cash value is less than the estate exemption amount ($1.5 million currently rising to $3.5 million in 2009) then there is no tax to make the gift.

You will, however, use up some of your estate tax exemption if the amount of the cash value exceeds your $11,000 annual exclusion ($22,000, if married). Keep in mind that the IRS will pull the death benefit back into your estate if you die within three years after gifting a policy. Some people will make the gift and then buy a three-year term policy to pay the estate taxes on the policy if they die within the three-year window.

Your other alternative is to sell the policy to your kids. When you sell the policy, the three-year rule discussed above does not apply. However, the IRS has set up another trap. The policy is exposed to the "transfer for value" rule. Since the policy was paid for, when the eventual death benefits are paid to the children, they will be taxable (normally, death benefits are tax free). The only way to escape the transfer for value rule is if you and your child are business partners. You can easily become partners by each buying a share in a publicly-traded master limited partnership (traded on the stock exchange).

Tricky? It can be. Consult a professional before removing a life insurance policy from your estate. However, if your estate exceeds the current exemption amount, then you should definitely remove the policy.

What is a Disclaimer?

Sometimes, people will delay their estate planning because they are not sure of the final choices they want to make. In such cases, having the beneficiaries know about a disclaimer can be very beneficial.

Take the example of a parent with a son who is a physician and doing well financially. The parent desires to leave funds to his son, but his son was well on his way to growing his own significant estate. If the parent was to leave additional assets to his son, he is only compounding his son's estate planning problem and making it more difficult to pass assets onto the grandchild. However, the parent does not want to leave the assets directly to the grandchild. This is where a disclaimer works wonderfully.

The parent can leave the assets to his son. However, at the time of inheritance, if the son would rather have the assets go directly to his son (the grandchild), he can "disclaim" the inheritance and the inheritance passes directly to the grandson. The assets never become part of the son's estate when the disclaimer is used. The inheritance is treated as if it passes from the grandparent to the grandchild (and generation skipping transfer tax could apply).

The disclaimer provides great flexibility in estate planning. The disclaimer could go to charity if the recipient so desires and the estate plan was so arranged, or the disclaimer can be used by one sibling to allocate assets to his poorer siblings. With some planning and knowledge of the disclaimer, very flexible estate plans can be constructed.

Trusts

When you hear the word "trust" in reference to estate planning, it could mean almost anything. A trust is simply an entity created by placing words on a paper. That entity becomes a legal being that often gets its own tax ID number and pays taxes like any other taxpayer.

Why do people create trusts? Because they allow savings of estate taxes and income taxes, as well as better control over assets. The different types of trusts are limited only by what you want to accomplish. Here are the typical types of trusts you want to know about:

Living Trusts—Assets placed in a living trust avoid probate. That's the principle benefit of a living trust and there are really no other tax or control benefits.

Irrevocable Trust—Assets placed in an irrevocable trust are outside of your estate and do not get included for your estate taxes. This is a powerful estate planning tool. Once you place an asset in an irrevocable trust, it can continue to grow and remains exempt from estate tax, no matter how large it gets. It's popular to place life insurance in these trusts (and then they are called "Irrevocable Life Insurance Trusts"), because life insurance death benefits are often many times the amount invested in the policy. This large death benefit is exempt from estate tax because it's out of your estate.

Qualified Personal Residence Trusts—This type of trust allows someone to place his or her residence in the trust and potentially pass the value of that residence to his or her heirs at a discounted value. This is popular with people who have large home values that they want to protect from estate taxes. You can continue to live in your house for the term of the trust (which you select). At the end of the term, the house passes out of your estate at a discounted value and you can rent it back from your heirs and continue to live there.

Grantor Retained Income Trust—Similar to the "Residence Trust" above, you place assets (stocks, bonds, investment real estate, etc.) into the trust. Then you receive an income stream and after a specified term of years, which you select, the assets pass to your beneficiaries at a discounted value.

2503c Trusts—These trusts hold assets for minors. Unlike the "Uniform Gift to Minors Trust" that many parents are familiar with, this type of trust allows you to place restrictions on the assets. For example, you can keep the assets in the trust until the child reaches a certain age or finishes college, etc.

We could fill a whole book on the different types of trusts. The important aspect is that if you have a desire regarding your assets, an experienced attorney can probably draft a trust to fulfill your desires.

INCOME PLANNING

Interest Rates at Twenty Year Lows

Seniors are more affected by declining interest rates than any other group, since many of them depend on income from investments. Some retirees still have a heavy reliance on CDs and treasury securities. These rates are now the lowest in more than 20 years! If investors keep depending on these sources, they may continue to find their income declining. This can only lead to personal financial disaster—living expenses keep increasing, while income decreases.

Is there a way out? Yes. The solution is the same as it has always been—invest long term. The appropriate investment time horizon for retirees is their life expectancy. A male investor age 70 has a life expectancy of 16 years.[53] That investor should be purchasing investments with a 16-year term, not six months or one year. If you have a choice, would you rather outlive your money or have your money outlive you?

---

[53] IRS Publiction 590, 2003.

Before judging this advice, consider if it is correct. If you had invested ten years ago or five years ago with your life expectancy as your time horizon, would you be better or worse off now? You would be better off because you would have invested in long-term fixed income securities and locked in attractive rates. You would have invested in blue chip stocks or funds that have appreciated considerably.

Unfortunately, many retired investors still invest out of fear, opting for short-term securities with low income payments. The result is what we see today—falling income and a worsening individual financial picture. So what can such retirees do now? Invest long term. There are still long-term CDs available that start out at 5.5% as of January 30, 2004 (CDs are FDIC insured, other investments are not).[54] Another alternative is federally-backed mortgage notes, which can pay 1-1.5% more than CDs. (Note that CDs are FDIC insured, while federally backed mortgage notes are federally backed, but not insured.) Another alternative is a lifetime immediate fixed annuity that provides an income you cannot outlive.[55]

Consult with an advisor experienced in working with retirees and learn about these and other ways to maintain your income even if rates are low.

---

[54] CUSIP# 74383UAJ4 callable CD 5.5%, call date 8/13/04, maturity 2/13/19.

[55] Purchase of mortgage notes and annuities may involve fees and commissions. Withdrawals from annuities prior to age 59½ subject to a 10% penalty. Annuities are backed by the claims-paying ability of the issuing insurance company.

Immediate Annuity Alternatives

The word "annuity" brings to mind different meanings for many investors. That's because there are different types of annuities designed for different purposes. The oldest of these is the immediate annuity, long used to generate a lifetime retirement income. The structure is well known, as follows:

The investor deposits a sum with an annuity company that agrees to pay a monthly amount for life, or a lesser amount to continue over the life of both spouses. The investor is provided with an income he or she cannot outlive.

Such an investment is useful for investors requiring income, qualifying for Medicaid (immediate annuities can be treated as an exempt asset), making lifetime payments to cover long-term care needs or paying long-term care insurance premiums.

The major drawback is an early death. In such a case, the annuity company keeps the funds and the income ends. This early-death financial risk has been a negative aspect for some investors. However, now there is a solution, as some annuity companies will guarantee return of the investment to heirs in the case of an early death. The feature is called "life payments with refund."

Some annuity holders have expressed concern that with fixed annuities, the monthly payment is fixed and may not keep pace with a rising cost of living. But some companies offer payments that rise over time.

What most people don't know is that most of the income is tax free. And immediate annuities often provide more income than other conservative investments.

Here's a hypothetical example.[56] A 76-year-old gentleman paid $50,000 in premium to an insurance company. He now receives $292 per month, every month. That's $3,504 each year of checks in the mail.

Regardless of how long a person lives, he gets his check every month. If he dies early, his beneficiaries will receive the $292 monthly payments if they have not been received for 20 years. (If the owner does not have beneficiaries and selects a straight life annuity, the monthly payments would be even higher at $434 per month.)

Real Estate

Rental property has always been a popular investment because of its appreciation potential and leverage. But in many parts of the country, it's a lousy cash flow investment.

Take a look at this hypothetical example. Say you own a rental home with a $250,000 value, free of debt. You receive rent of $1,200 per month. After expenses (including those periodic expenses of replacing the roof, adding an air conditioner, painting), you net $800 per month. If you sold the property, you would receive

---

[56] Rates from average of 16 immediate annuity companies using the calculator at www.immediateannuity.com.

$188,000 after taxes. Now let's put these numbers together. Your net $800 per month ($9,600 per year) on equity of $188,000 (the amount you would have if you sold the property). That's an annual cash return of 5.1%. Is that cash return worth getting calls to fix the plumbing, chasing late rent checks or needing to evict tenants?

Does it really make sense to own real estate? Yes, you would answer, because the real estate appreciates. But on a cash flow basis alone, this property has a poor return. As investors age, many become more interested in spendable cash flow and less interested in appreciation. (By the way—people sometimes incorrectly prepare the above analysis based on the amount they originally paid for the property. To correctly see what you are earning, you must use the current equity because that's the amount of money you could invest elsewhere.)

If you want to increase your cash flow, real estate is not the right investment in many areas of the country (the value of real estate is in its appreciation potential). An income-oriented investor, who wants to get rid of the hassles of real estate ownership, would be better off with good quality fixed income investments, which may pay 8% or more.

This recommendation may be hard to accept if you have owned a property for many years. The analysis often shows that the cash flow is poor and monthly income could be significantly enhanced if the real estate equity were invested in other ways.

TAX STRATEGIES

Lower Your Tax

Many taxpayers think that the capital gains rate was cut to 15% in the last round of tax cuts. That's right, but it's only part of the story. Many investors qualify for an even lower 5% capital gains rate. How do you get this lower rate?

The 5% capital gains rate applies to taxpayers who are in the 15% marginal tax bracket (e.g. married couples and singles with taxable incomes below $56,800 and $28,400, respectively). While some taxpayers are consistently above these levels, they should not overlook a chance to lower their tax bracket for one year in order to take advantage of a lower capital gains rate.

For example, some people live comfortably on pension and Social Security income. They have been in the 28% federal tax bracket for many years. Because of some recent purchase of property and new mortgage deductions, their tax bracket has dropped to 15%, temporarily. While the 15% regular tax bracket applies to them, they can sell some appreciated assets and enjoy the 5% capital gains rate.

Let's say a retired couple has $60,000 of income, but they have heavy deductions that year, reducing their taxable income to $30,000. (Other ways to reduce taxable income include using a short-term annuity or tax-free bonds.) Since the 15% tax bracket extends up to $56,800 for married tax payers, filing jointly, they could use up to $26,800 ($56,800 minus $30,000) of capital gains and have them taxed at 5%. Another way to enjoy the 5% capital gains rate involves gifting stock or mutual funds to a grandchild (who is in the 15% tax bracket), and having the capital gains upon sale taxed at only 5% to him or her.

This may be an opportunity for you to cut your capital gains tax by two-thirds from 15% to 5%, but remember, you need to time the sale of your securities correctly.

Tax Loss Planning

Every year, thousands of investors in stocks and mutual funds miss the benefit of tax loss selling—when an investor has the government share his or her investment losses by reducing his or her taxes.

If you bought a stock at 20 and it's now 15, even if you plan to hold it for the long term, sell it now! By selling, you can report a $5.00 loss per share on your tax return. Take a deduction (or offset other stock gains) and reduce your tax bill or receive a refund. You can then buy the shares back in 31 days and keep them as long as you like.

If you just sit there with your paper loss and December 31 passes, the government will not share the loss with you. You must actually make a sale to capture the tax benefit. If you miss this each year, you throw away a tax savings and pay more taxes than necessary. Make it a ritual to sell your losers each December and have the IRS share the loss with you.

Annuity Taxation

A woman recently came to see me about converting her annuity to a life insurance policy. Her husband had died four-and-a-half years ago and the annuity had been left to accumulate. Unfortunately, the agent had written the annuity so that the children were the beneficiaries. The wife had no claim to this money! Moreover, the entire interest in the annuity ($280,000) must be distributed within five years of the owner's death (IRC section (72)(s)(1)). Therefore, since the end of the five years was near, the entire annuity soon had to be distributed to the children and the tax bill would exceed $50,000!

Had the original agent understood what he was doing, he would have made the wife the beneficiary or the husband and wife joint owners or joint annuitants. This lack of knowledge is causing this family a large premature tax bill.

Here's the point: please obtain annuities from someone who understands the tax ramifications. Has your annuity been written correctly?

Yearly Tax Review

Although you'd like your accountant to give you tax tips, many do not. They simply prepare your tax return and let you go to accumulate another tax bill for the next year. If you seriously want to cut your income taxes, go see your accountant or financial advisor before December 31. Here are the kinds of savings you can uncover:

- Mutual funds, which are generating too much short-term gains (taxed at higher rates) rather than long-term gains.
- Higher than necessary IRA distributions.
- Unnecessary payment of taxes on Social Security income.
- Opportunities to increase current income.
- Opportunities to sell securities and avoid capital gains.
- Opportunities to remove money from IRAs or pension plans at substantially reduced taxes.
- Improper investment of bypass trust assets, where one spouse has died.

If you are tired of paying more tax than necessary and want to do something about it, you can stop the waste. Don't think that your accountant has given you the answers unless you ask! Will your 2004 tax return look like this?

NEW 2004 FEDERAL SHORT FORM	
1. Amount You Earned	$ _____
2. Send in Amount on Line 1	$ _____

Family Partnership

For years, the wealthy have been using estate planning techniques that may be unfamiliar to many people who could benefit from the same techniques. For example, if estate taxes are a concern, read how you can use a simple device, the "Family Partnership," to slice your tax bill.

Let's say that you and your spouse own a farm with a $1 million value. If it is left in your estate, this property could be burdened with estate taxes up to 48% of the value. Wouldn't it be nice if you could "shrink" the value for estate tax purposes? The family partnership can do that for you.

All you have to do is ask an attorney to draw up a family partnership document, which creates a family partnership (just like you had the attorney draw up a living trust document, which created a living trust). The farm now gets deeded to the family partnership. This is a non-taxable event. (Per the IRS, a transfer to partnership in return for partnership interest is not taxable.) In return for donating the farm to your family partnership, you and your spouse receive 100 partnership "units" in return as evidence of your ownership in the partnership. Think of these units as shares.

Each year, you begin gifting some of these partnership units to your children. You might think that each unit is worth $10,000 ($1 million divided by 100 units). But here's the best part. For estate tax purposes, the farm inside the family partnership is worth less— let's say $700,000 in this example, and each partnership unit is worth (for tax purposes) only $7,000 in the hands of your children. (The actual discounted value is ascertained by an appraiser who is experienced in setting discounts for family partnership assets.) Why is there a discount?

The IRS allows a valuation discount for two reasons. The first is "lack of marketability." The IRS agrees that the units you gift to your children are virtually unsellable to anyone. Secondly, your children have no control over the farm. This is called the "minority interest" discount. As a result, the farm value for estate tax purposes is now only $700,000! You have just wiped out $300,000 of estate value (a potential estate tax savings of $144,000) by forming a family partnership.[57]

But the partnership has other benefits. Let's say someone falls off a ladder working on your house and sues you. Your assets in the partnership are protected from suits and creditors. (Claimants only have "charging orders" in states that have adopted the uniform act.) Even though the partnership units may be gifted away over time to your children (to remove the value from your estate), you can remain the lifetime general partner. That means you are always the boss. You decide how the farm gets managed, whether to sell it or borrow against it or whatever decisions you choose to make. It's all in your control.

For a combination of estate tax savings, protection

---

[57] "Discounts in the range of 30% are fairly conservative, but some aggressive advisors push this number to the 50% range." R. Mintz, Asset Protection Specialists, www.rjmintz.com. Estate of Dailey vs. Commission, TC memo 2001-263 is one. In this case, the court allowed a 40% total discount on an FLP containing marketable securities, www.vlwcpa.com.

from creditors and ease of estate distribution, a family partnership can be a very powerful tool.

What is a Gift Annuity?

Periodically, someone who sold some stock or property earlier in the year wants to know what he or she can do to offset the large tax bill created by the sale. While planning before the sale provides a lot more options, there is still a way to save tax after the sale with a gift annuity.

A gift annuity results by making a gift to a qualified charity, but you get income from the gift for life and you get an immediate tax deduction that can be used to shelter the tax from your real estate or stock sale. Let's look at an example.[58]

Suppose Mr. Jones, age 70, sells a property for $100,000 that has been fully depreciated. Let's simplify and assume a tax due of $15,000. Can he shelter this tax? Yes.

He can set up a gift annuity. He contributes the $100,000 of his proceeds and receives a $6,500 annual income for life (of which 59% is considered a tax-free return of principal and not taxed until the gift is recovered). In addition, he receives a tax deduction of $38,660 right away. Look what he has accomplished:

- He has offset part of his capital gains tax with a

---

[58] Figures based on IRS Section 7520 discount rate 4.8% and on American Council on gift annuity rates in effect 2/2/04.

tax deduction of $38,660.
- He generates a lifetime income of $6,500 annually, partially tax free.
- He benefits his favorite charity.

It gets even better if Mr. Jones does not need the income today. He can defer it. If he defers the income for ten years, his income will increase to $14,647 per year and the tax deduction increases to $88,883.

This same technique can be used to shelter taxes from an IRA or retirement plan distribution, while still providing an annual income. Since the annual income from a gift annuity is based on age, the older the contributor, the larger the income.

If interested, a qualified advisor can provide a quotation of income and tax savings for your situation.

Sell Real Estate and Avoid the Tax

Do you have a single-family rental property that was purchased years ago with big gains? It may not be convenient, but if you and your spouse move in and live there for two years, you can then sell and avoid tax on the first $500,000 of gain ($250,000 for a single taxpayer).[59] In fact, you could unload a whole portfolio of rental houses, and possibly do so tax free, by living in each for two years before selling.

Do you own an apartment building that you no longer want to care for and want to go live in France for a year? You can exchange the apartment building for

---

[59] IRA Publication 17, 2003.

any other investment property, such as ownership of say, a McDonald's location (a hypothetical example to illustrate the concept).[60] Under a triple net lease, McDonald's (or the franchisee) take total responsibility for the property. Your monthly rent check can be deposited in your bank account as you travel through the Bordeaux region. (Note: when you exchange real estate, you do not actually exchange one property for another. You sell your property and those funds go immediately into escrow for the new property you are purchasing. Such an exchange is tax free.)

Maybe it's time to get rid of those 500 acres of farm land that doesn't make any money. You can donate it to a charitable trust, and as the trustee, sell it tax free. Then you can invest the money as you see fit in stocks or bonds, receive a hypothetical 8% payout (or a rate you select based on IRS limits), lifetime annual income and have the property out of your hair and out of your estate (and at the same time create a nice donation for your favorite charities when you pass on and a nice tax deduction for yourself).

The tax rules provide flexibility when it comes to real estate. It's easy to harvest profits and avoid taxes in many situations.

Mutual Fund Turnover Costs

Many investors own mutual funds, but few of them realize how much they really earn after taxes. Here's a little insight from *Creating Equity* by John Bowen. In a study commissioned by Charles Schwab and conducted

---

[60] IRS Section 1031.

by John B. Shoven, professor of Economics at Stanford University, and Joel M. Dickson, a Stanford Ph.D. candidate, taxable distributions were found to have an impact on the rates of return of many well-known retail equity mutual funds.

The study measured the performance of 62 equity funds for the 30-year period from 1963 through the end of 1992. It found that the high-tax investor who reinvested only after-tax distributions would end up with accumulated wealth per dollar invested equal to less than half (45%) of the funds' published performances. An investor in the middle-tax bracket would see only 55% of the performance published by the funds.

Another study, by Robert H. Jeffrey and Robert D. Arnott, published in the *Journal of Portfolio Management*, concluded that extremely low portfolio turnover can be a factor in improving a fund's potential after-tax performance. Asset class funds typically have very low portfolio turnover, which translates into less frequent trading and, therefore, may result in lower capital gains. Low turnover also may benefit shareholders by holding down trading cost.

In plain English, the above studies indicate that you can lose a lot of your returns from mutual funds to taxes and that funds with high turnover tend to generate higher taxes for you. You can find out how tax-efficient your funds are by consulting information services available in many local libraries or consulting a financial advisor experienced in the tax issues of mutual funds.

Lower Your Capital Gains Taxes

There are at least four ways to eliminate or defer capital gains tax upon the sale of an asset. These ideas are outlined for you below.

1. Before the sale, donate the asset to a charitable remainder trust and have the trust sell it and then provide the income to you.

2. Donate the appreciated asset to a personal foundation and have the foundation employ you or your family members (in addition to doing good works in the community). Take a tax deduction for the donation.

3. In the case of stock, you can exchange shares of stock for an interest in a specialized small business investment company (SSBIC)—essentially a mutual fund of small company stocks. Thus, you can diversify what may be too much money in one stock for an interest in several, and thereby reduce your risk. If these new shares are held until death, no capital gains tax is paid.[61]

4. In the case of real estate, an unwanted old apartment building can be exchanged for a chain location on a triple-net lease (e.g. McDonald's). You eliminate all management headaches, as the chain has full responsibility for the property. You get a nice rental income check each month and

---

[61] See limitations, IRS Publication 550, Chapter 4.

if the property is held until death, there is no capital gains tax.

Want a Significant Tax Deduction?

If you would like to generate a significant tax deduction, consider giving away your house, but don't move out!

Many charities will work an agreement with you to take your house as a bequest when you pass away, and yet provide you with the charitable deduction this year. You continue to live in your house for your lifetime, yet have the benefit of saving tax dollars this year (and possibly into future years). So if you have been thinking about a significant charitable contribution, this may be a painless alternative for making a contribution to your favorite charity. If you leave your house through your will or trust, you get no income tax savings. If you make the arrangements now, then you could save tens of thousands of income tax dollars. That's money you can spend now.

You can achieve some of the estate tax benefits and leave the house to your heirs, at a discounted estate value, by using the Qualified Personal Resident Trust (QPRT). This type of trust splits the value of your residence into two parts—the value represented by the time you will live in the house during your lifetime and the "remainder" value that you leave to your heirs. The present value of this remainder interest can be a heavily discounted figure for estate tax purposes. The smaller your estate is calculated to be, the lower the estate tax. Consult a legal advisor for more information about this option.

How to Lower Your Social Security Taxes

As retirees well know, the federal government takes back part of your Social Security through taxes. Depending on your level of income, the tax can be levied on up to 85% of your Social Security benefits. Can you beat the tax? Yes, many can and here's how.

The general approach is to defer income. Deferred income does not appear on your tax return, it is not part of your taxable income. Therefore, deferred income can reduce the amount included for the Social Security benefit tax calculation.[62] Tax-free income will not reduce the tax on your Social Security income, because tax-free income is included in the IRS Social Security tax calculation. Here are your sources of tax-deferred income:

Deferred Annuities.
Some investors shy away from annuities, because they have the mistaken impression that all annuities tie up their money. In fact, annuities are issued in terms as short as one year. Reinvested interest is all deferred and such an investment can reduce or eliminate the tax on Social Security income.

Certain Zero Coupon Bonds.
There are a few issues of corporate zero coupon bonds that have tax-deferred status. (Even though E-bonds are tax-deferred, the IRS specifically includes them when calculating the taxes on your Social Security income.)

[62] IRS Publication 17, 2003.

Below you will find an example of the effect on taxes for receiving interest from CDs versus tax-free bonds and annuities. (Note that CDs are FDIC insured and other investments are not.)

Table 8.1
Effect on Taxes for Receiving Interest from CDs vs. Annuities and Tax-Free Bonds

	Scenario #1 Interest from CDs	Scenario #2 Interest from Tax-Free Bonds	Scenario #3 Fixed Annuity Interest (Not Distributed)
Interest	$10,000	$10,000	($10,000)
Pensions	$25,000	$25,000	$25,000
Social Security Income	$20,000	$20,000	$20,000
Total Income	$55,000	$55,000	$45,000
Social Security Subject to Tax	$6,850	$6,850	$1,500
Adjusted Gross Income	$41,850	$31,850	$26,500
Total Federal Tax	$2,956	$1,456	$903

The figures above are for a hypothetical married couple receiving Social Security income and how their tax liability changes under various investment scenarios, substituting a deferred annuity or municipal bond for a CD. Note that CDs are protected by FDIC insurance and other investments are not. Figures are calculated by TurboTax 1040 2003. See Appendix A located at the end of this book to see the basis for comparison.

Can a Trust Help with Taxes?

There are as many kinds of trusts as there are flavors of ice cream. Many can help save taxes. Here are a few ideas:

Personal Residence Trust

Think of your house as having two portions of value—the time you spend living in your home for the rest of your life and the value of the home after you die that you leave to your heirs (the residual value). It's the second portion that is part of your estate and potentially subject to estate taxes. The IRS allows you to give that portion to your heirs now at a discounted value to potentially save estate taxes.

If you are familiar with the concept of "present value," you know that one dollar, 20 years from now, is only worth 45 cents today (discounted at 4%). Therefore, you can place that discounted residual value in a trust now and remove it from your estate. If you are alive at the end of the trust term, you will need to pay your heirs rent to live in your house because technically, you will no longer have any right to ownership or right to reside there. If the trust outlives you, you have potentially saved a fortune in estate tax.

Grantor-Retained Income Trust

This type of trust works similar to the above except that rather than placing your house in a trust, you place other assets—stocks, funds, investment property. Again, you remove the future value of the asset from your estate today.

Private Annuity Trust

This works for passing real estate to heirs and deferring capital gains tax. For example, you could take an apartment building that you own and place it in the trust in exchange for a note. The trust sells the building (and owes no capital gains because the basis and the sales price are the same). The trust invests the money and makes payments to you on the note. You pay capital gains tax as you receive each payment and spread the taxes over years.

At your passing, the note is extinguished and the assets in the trust pass to your heirs, estate tax free.

These are just three ideas using trusts that can keep the IRS away, increase your financial security (assets in trust are usually protected from your creditors) and increase benefits to family.

CONSEQUENCES OF USING THE WRONG STRATEGY

As discussed earlier, retirees tend to become overly conservative with their investment strategies as they move into retirement, and for good reason. Most retirees have a sense that if their assets are going to have to provide income for long retirement periods, they had better protect those assets from loss. To most retirees, that generally means more conservative investments. Thus, instead of having their portfolios properly allocated, taking into account the need for both liquidity (income) and growth, many of you will tend to invest far too heavily in the fixed income portion of the portfolio because it seems "less risky." In the extreme, you might even invest everything in fixed-income accounts to make your portfolio "as safe as possible."

However, if we are successful in defining risk for you as the likelihood of not meeting their retirement income expectations, it is obvious that becoming too conservative too soon may very well be the riskiest thing they can do. In fact, in order to make the same $500,000 in the earlier example last for 30 years if it was all invested in fixed income investments earning a historical rate of return of about 5.5 percent, it would take a reduction in income of about 25 percent per year, or an increase in beginning retirement assets of about

32 percent! This is clearly a very risky way to manage retirement assets!

Clearly, investing too conservatively during retirement is not a good idea. However, the flip side of the coin, investing too aggressively, is just as risky and inadvisable. Ultimately, as we have already shown, retirees should try to invest neither too conservatively nor too aggressively and always keep in mind the need for both income and growth over longer and longer retirement periods. Of course, the most aggressive investment posture would be to stay fully invested in the stock market throughout retirement and simply plan to sell stocks periodically for income as needed.

This, too, is a very risky retirement management technique for a number of reasons, all of which are based upon the same fundamental problem. That problem concerns the fact that selling stocks out of a portfolio that is fluctuating in value requires the sale of more shares when the market is down, and fewer shares when the market is up, to generate the same amount of income. In essence, using this strategy forces an investor into dollar-cost averaging out of the stock market, which is just as negative as dollar-cost averaging into the market is positive. We all know that we should sell more shares when they are up and fewer shares when they are down. The process of planning to sell stocks periodically to meet the need for retirement income will lock us into exactly the opposite approach, which is a fundamentally (and often fatally) flawed investment strategy. It is one of the most dangerous things we could do besides investing too conservatively.

Historical evidence shows just how risky it is for a retiree to stay fully invested in equities while planning to sell stocks periodically for income. A well-known study conducted by three professors at Trinity University, generally referred to as the Trinity Study, concluded that over all 30-year time periods between 1946 and 1997, a portfolio consisting of 100 percent stocks would have been able to provide six percent inflation adjusted income only 57 percent of the time, if an investor was dollar-cost-averaging out of the market on a monthly basis. That means that 43 percent of the time, retirees would have run out of money before the end of their lives. For a portfolio consisting of 50 percent stocks and 50 percent bonds, the "success rate" drops to 35 percent. These are terrible odds, and most retirees who understand these realities will be very reluctant to manage their portfolios in this way.

Thus, once retirees understand the realities and the alternatives, most will choose to do it the right way! They will choose not to invest too conservatively and they will choose not to invest to aggressively. They will put themselves into a retirement management strategy that will allow them to navigate all of the uncertainties they are sure to face over a 30-year retirement period. So, what then do we really mean by navigating?

In a typical case, we might create a plan to spend our first income leg over an initial 10-year holding period, allow equity investments to grow at higher expected rates of return in the stock market and then use the appreciated equity accounts to fund subsequent period income legs.

Realistically, the actual investment results in the stock market could be much different than expected. For example, equity markets could be much better than anticipated in the first few years, as would have happened recently. Consequently, our equity accounts might be worth as much after three or four years as we expected them to be worth after 10 years. At this point, we might take some of the excess value out of the stock market to create another income leg (way ahead of schedule) to augment the six or seven years remaining in our initial income leg. By doing so, we would significantly extend the amount of income (liquidity) we have reserved in our portfolio. We would also be extending the length of our next holding period as it relates to the assets we leave invested in the stock market. We would now have more years of income set aside and longer holding periods (and therefore less risk) relating to the assets remaining in equities. All in all, we would be much better off then when we started!

However, it would be wishful thinking to expect that things will always start out on such a positive note. Market realities might leave us with less than we expected to have at the end of our first holding period. What would we do then? Once again, we would need to navigate.

For example, even though our plans might call for the sale of Blue Chip stocks, it may be that Growth stocks have done better than expected and that it would be preferable to sell them to create the next income leg. If all equity markets happen to be down at the same time, we might simply choose not to sell as many equities and defer the building of the next income leg to a more opportune time. Instead, we might choose to sell just as many shares as necessary to fund our income needs until markets recover. Often, in the face of challenges such as these, we might choose to cut back on income for a while. On the other hand, we might choose to utilize cash reserves that had been stashed away for this very situation. The idea is that a good retirement plan should provide the maximum amount of flexibility to respond to the changing circumstances that every retiree is bound to encounter over longer retirement periods.

Given a diversified portfolio of stocks, bonds, CDs, annuities, life insurance, etc., along with the holding periods needed to make well-timed stock market transactions, a retiree can press forward into the unknown with a great deal of comfort and financial control. With a little creativity, there are almost as many ways to approach future investment challenges as there are individuals in retirement.

Because there are so many options open to each individual, both during the planning process and throughout retirement, it is important to be working with a professional who can help establish reasonable goals and plans and, perhaps most importantly, help navigate those plans. There is no greater source of value during retirement than an advisor who really understands a client's goals, who has the skill and experience to help navigate changing circumstances in "real time" and who can help address a wide array of closely related concerns, such as income tax, insurance and estate planning. Only with a good education will you really understand that your goal is not to outperform others, but to help make sure that you have an income you will not outlive.[63]

---

[63] This entire chapter is from *Managing Money During Retirement - A New Way to Navigate Changing Realities* by Paul A. Grangaard, is reprinted (in part) with the publisher's permission from the Journal of Retirement Planning, Vol. 3 No. 3, a bimonthly journal published by CCH INCORPORATED. Copying or distribution without the publisher's permission is prohibited.

ACKNOWLEDGEMENTS

Barry Picker, CPA/PFS, CFP
Victor Finmann, Esq.
Robert Keebler, CPA, MST
Natalie Choate, Esq.
Ed Slott, CPA
Stephan Leimberg, Esq.
Larry Klein, CPA
Seymour Goldberg, CPA, Esq.
Thomas Gau, CPA
Steven Lockwood, JD, LLM
Bill Bachrach, CSP

BOOK SUMMARY

As I said in the introduction, money's not that important. It's important only to the extent that it allows you to enjoy what really matters to you. Not having to worry about your finances is critical to having a life that excites you, nurtures those you love, and fulfills your highest aspirations.

You deserve the Peace of Mind you have always hoped for and Compass™ will let you achieve that. Having Peace of Mind will allow you to go to sleep at night knowing you are prepared for tomorrow. Ultimately, Peace of Mind comes from eliminating financial stress out of your life and giving you the ability to enjoy retirement.

Here are a few parting words of advice if you aren't able to find a Trusted Advisor and use Compass™. First, ignore much of what you read in the financial press. Most of it is just hype. One radio show host commented that on his radio show he used phrases like " Dow soars," Unemployment worsens," "Interest rates rise." He said he always had a long-term view, but if he went on the air and advised this every day, no one would listen to his advice. He had to make each day sound exciting!

Secondly, make a plan, stick to it and enjoy life. There are always going to be terrorism, wars, gas shortages, and bombings. Your plan should always ignore these. I remember the invasion of Kuwait like it was yesterday. The stock market plummeted; people were scared of the outcome, possible disruptions in oil flow and a resulting recession. I advised investors to ignore this and follow their plan and not the news.

I will not wish you luck because investing well has nothing to do with luck. I do wish you smart choices based on sound principles. If I can be of any help to you, I welcome the opportunity to help you. I would be delighted to answer any questions you might have.

You can call me directly or write down you questions and send them to me. Take care and God Bless.

Steven Casto
11414 W. Center Rd., Suite 344
Omaha, NE 68144

Phone: 402-333-8751
Fax: 402-333-8753
E-mail: Steve@stevecasto.com
Website: www.stevecasto.com

Compass™ has positively improved

thousands of seniors' lives.

ABOUT STEVEN CASTO

Steve is a nationally known financial author and is a well-known retirement educator in the Omaha, Nebraska area. He has developed a specialty in working with seniors and those about to retire who want to protect their principal and ensure that their money lasts. Steve helps people avoid the most common mistakes made by most retirees.

Steve is a Certified Senior Advisor, which required him to take a twenty-two-section course of study and pass a rigorous exam proving his comprehensive knowledge of personal retirement issues as they apply to seniors. He has been issued an A+ for business Ethics by the National Verification Agency. Steve was listed in The National Register's Who's Who in 2003. Steve has helped countless seniors cut their income taxes significantly, maximize income and eliminate the fear of outliving their money.

Steve and his wife Kim, who is CEO of Ladybug Floral & Gifts, live in the Blair area.

APPENDIX A

Basis for Comparison

	CDs	Fixed Annuities	Municipal Bonds
Fees, commissions	No	Yes, plus surrender charges	Yes, upon purchase and sale
Liquidity	Yes, with early withdrawal penalty	Surrender charges within term if surrendered	Maybe poor
Fluctuation	None	No, unless MVA feature applies when surrendered prior to term	Gain or loss if sold before maturity
Interest Taxed	Ordinary income as it accrues	Taxed as ordinary income, penalty for withdrawals prior to age 59½	Exempt from federal, possibly exempt from state unless private activity bond and possibly subject to AMT
Guarantee	FDIC insured	Guaranteed by the claims-paying ability of the insurance company	Guaranteed by the issuing municipality, agency or entity